MARKED MEN

by

Al and Jayne Houghton

Marked Men

Copyright © 2007 by Al and Jayne Houghton

ISBN: 978-1-59352-325-1

Published by:

CSN BOOKS

7287 Birchcreek Road

San Diego, CA 92119

Toll-free: 1-866-757-9953

Dedication

Marked Men is dedicated to Gabriel Jonathan Houghton and his generation who in their lifetime face a much different world than their grandparents who benefited from all those willing to bleed and die in winning World War II.

May those of us who know the value of fighting and winning war, never cease in our discipleship until we have reproduced God's heart for war in their generation knowing that a failure to do so may well cost a nation the freedom for which Christ died!

Acknowledgments

Wherever prophetic truth is prepared for publication, wisdom directs intercession for gathering the multitude of counselors necessary for birthing a refining fire that may be received. I'm very thankful to the Lord for assembling such, whose contributions dramatically shaped the development of this manuscript.

I wish to acknowledge and thank:

My wife Jayne for her contribution of adding warm oil which will greatly facilitate digestion of hard words and be obvious to all who read this work. Her faithful support through many years of speaking truths, where "ears to hear" did not always exist, cannot be measured in utterable words!

Steve Hake, whose acute analytical assessment, honed over years of writing America's finest Math Curriculum, accurately assessed our global spiritual future.

Pastor Brian Harrison, whose "Baptist brain" demanded absolute historical accuracy with many exhortations to simplify and clarify. Brian's input has been invaluable and he would make every "Berean" proud.

Pastor Connie Duffy for her forceful assertion that in order to uphold the gravity due the title, every aspect of God's marking process should be related and clearly enumerated. Her perceptive and prophetic insight into essential marks contributed greatly to the "fullness" of this work.

Pastor Larry Brewer, whose former life as an attorney proved invaluable in crossing "t's" and dotting "i's" and encouraging me to go for the "jugular." Prophetic attorneys make wonderful friends.

Don King (not the fight promoter) whose "faith trained brain" proved essential in refining concepts with which many believers are not familiar. His evangelistic heart wonderfully assisted in reviewing and rephrasing comments some might have considered "overly pointed."

My "California Corrections" Parole Board Chairwoman trained secretary, *Jo Lees*, who encouraged keeping the "razor's edge" and whose diligent attention to detail eliminated many errors, making the publication process much smoother, not to mention her insistence on incarceration until this project was complete.

Shan Gastineau, whose encouragement quoting Napoleon almost brought out the cannons.

Pat Gastineau for her "kinder-gentler" suggestions.

Pastor Joe McIntyre, whose unwavering commitment to live what he preaches also manifests in his editorial skills which are outstanding!

The list and depth of contributors is so large, I probably should be referred to as editor instead of author. With great appreciation, this work is offered and dedicated to the preparation of the next generation, that they may find and fulfill all the vision of taking cities and nations, just as God has shown it to their spiritual parents.

Table of Contents

CHAPTER 1

Overcoming Prophetic Myths

Marked Men began in April of 1986 after an extended season of prayer. Only twice in all my years of interacting with the Lord, have I ever heard what seemed like the audible voice of God. The first instance helped me decide to turn from pursuing a career with the airlines and embrace the call to full-time ministry. The second time was a command so forceful that occasionally I still hear it today: "PREPARE MY PEOPLE FOR PERSECUTION!" Today's world is much different from the one in which I first heard those words. Who could have foreseen the rise of militant Islam and the genocidal slaughter of Christians in so many nations? Jesus said we would "know them by their fruit" and Islam has produced a theology for Hitlers, justification for an Antichrist and fulfillment for John 16:2: "... the time is coming that whoever kills you will think that he offers God service." That time is here and how do we respond? Leadership denial does not prepare a nation politically nor does it prepare a generation biblically.

One of America's greatest educators recently noted, "Other nations across the globe are feeling the affects of militant Islam. Indonesia has its hands full suppressing jihadist activity. Thailand suffers fatal terrorist attacks almost daily. India is experiencing more and more violence. Almost all of Europe is intimidated by growing, unassimilated Muslims. If a nation on the globe does not face an internal or neighboring Islamic problem, then it is at least dependent on Mid-east oil and does not want to offend its energy provider. This is a worldwide problem that is shifting from festering to seething. I cannot envision a set of circumstances that would turn down the heat. On the contrary, the course from seething to disruption seems inevitable. The timeline is unclear, but it does seem like time strengthens the enemy's hand."

In the two world wars of the twentieth century, nations aligned against nations. What is shaping up in the twenty-first century does not just pit nation against nation, but kingdom against kingdom.

As we progressively move toward the culmination of the "last days," God both prepares and marks His people, enabling them to accomplish their pre-assigned purposes contributing to a harvest of nations and blaze a trail of testimonies that should exceed those of the early church. Are we ready to stand alone as God's voice to the nations? Are we ready to face persecution that parallels and exceeds that of the early church?

Volumes have been written about Satan's end-time mark, even though it is only a counterfeit, whereas very little has been penned about God's equipping of the generation that will constitute the glorious—without spot, wrinkle, or blemish—double anointing church! This book is about how to traverse the distance from where we are now, as the people of the Lord, to where God wants to take us. Much of the church is a "bless-me club" far from ready to face demonized hoards. The journey is not for the faint of heart, but for all who can receive mercy and grace to become exceedingly courageous. It is for those who more comfortably relate to Joshua and Caleb's position informing Israel of what they saw, even though it was not the popular or majority opinion.

Nearly everyone knows the significance of 666, but how many believers are familiar with the nine elements constituting God's end-time mark for His people? The ultimate goal is to birth a generation of believers who recognize and pursue all nine elements of God's sealing process, with the same fervor Charismatics pursue developing the nine gifts and evangelicals seek the nine fruit. The New Testament presents a picture of two distinct groups in the last days, each with their appointed leaders locked in deadly confrontation, manifesting the full character and nature of the God to which they adhere. Each group wears the seal of their God. In John 16:2, Jesus warned, "They will put you out of the synagogues; yes, the time is coming that whoever kills you will think that he offers God service." Islam provides the theology of which Jesus spoke! Our forefathers who bled and died for freedom of religion must be mystified that a generation could live under their flag and be so deceived as to think what they died for could include radical Islam. Extending freedom to the radically demonized intent on destroying you by growing terrorists under the banner of church is far from what they intended. Freedom of religion meant freedom for Christianity not freedom for demons. Let's make sure we are thoroughly equipped and ready to face such demon-possessed people. We must **know** what fills our hearts. God marks all who determine, despite the cost, to stay on His path.

Most Christians can identify the number of Satan's sign (666), but how many of us can name one of the true marks for believers? God's marks are: 1) spiritual action against evil (overcoming tolerance) 2) fullness 3) Holy Spirit with signs 4) adversity 5) His name 6) justice (mish-pawt) 7) purity 8) faithfulness 9) intimacy. Do we view any of these as essential elements of preparation for the end-time church?

The prophets saw a glorious victorious church. Isaiah prophesied in chapter 60 such a dramatic season of visitation, that the pattern of evangelism would change so there would be little need to go to the world, because the masses would come to the glory displayed by the rising church.

The prophet Haggai saw a season where God's presence was so powerful, the spirit of mammon was dispossessed. God promised to manifest His authority by the glory of the latter house eclipsing the former. The prophet Joel surely agreed with Isaiah and Haggai when he said the rain would come down for us—the former and the latter simultaneously, releasing an overflowing harvest. He even used the word "full" to describe this harvest. The Old Testament prophet Zechariah must have seen the same things as his fellow prophets because he encouraged us to "Ask the Lord for rain in the time of the latter rain," promising God would pour it forth.

Ephesians 4 reveals God's heart for every church member to develop their assigned gifting. The full measure of the stature of Jesus Christ resident in the local church is only reached through five different ministry gifts. Input from the prophets saw such a season and Jesus promised to fulfill it! The question seems to be, "How fast can we grow into this army by studying a counterfeit?" It does not take a multitude to transform the local church, just a few good men and women willing to invest in an eternal vision. God gives a very special reward to all who pursue His prophetic purposes. When we embrace biblical vision, carry it, believe for it, share it with our children and sacrifice for its realization, whether we see the manifestation in our generation or not, God rewards us with a unique Hebrews 11 and 12 status—a view from the balcony of heaven in the cloud of witnesses.

Spiritual Pioneers

The Holy Spirit offers participation in Abraham's path and pattern (a high honor), but it seems many more reject than accept, possibly for a lack of understanding. Abraham was called to pioneer spiritually by embracing a prophetic promise never realized in his day. Hebrews 11:9 and 10 say:

> By faith he sojourned in the land of promise as in a foreign country, dwelling in tents with Isaac and Jacob, the heirs with him of the same promise; for he waited for the city which has foundations, whose builder and maker is God.

Abraham's actions pleased God even though he never realized the promises in his lifetime. Hebrews 11:13-16 states:

> These all died in faith, not having received the promises, but having seen them afar off were assured of them, embraced them, and confessed that they were strangers and pilgrims on the earth. For those who say such things declare plainly that they seek a homeland. And truly if they had called to mind that country from which they had come out, they would have had opportunity to return. But now they desire a better, that is, a heavenly country. Therefore God is not ashamed to be called their God, for He has prepared a city for them.

When the Holy Spirit leads us to embrace prophetic vision, our choice to accept may bring great adversity, but the simple act of continuing day by day, week by week, month by month, and year by year is the real essence of Hebrews 11 faith and makes God proud. When we say "yes" to Him, we join the tribe of wandering spiritual pioneers who look for a city "...whose builder and maker is God." He never asks us to walk without mistakes, faults and failures, just that we keep walking. The personal choices we make result in Him being either pleased or ashamed to be identified with us. Abraham pleased God by using faith to subdue his own flesh, and the Lord redeemed his poor choices. We live in a generation which seems much more interested in spending its spiritual energy and faith for personal benefit. Hebrews 11 warns that such an attitude makes God ashamed when we publicly name Jesus as Lord! Abraham pleased God by using his faith on his flesh to become a pioneer and obey the heavenly call. When Abraham lifted the knife to slay Isaac, by faith he overcame his natural inclination and became "...the father of all those who believe...." What is our generation fathering?

The declaration of Hebrews 12:1: "Therefore we also, since we are witnesses..." identifies a unique status for those who overcome adversity and plant the vision in the next generation. This verse seems to indicate all those who embraced prophetic vision, carried it, pursued it and planted it, but never realized it in their lifetime, qualify to view from eternity each successive generation until they see the one which will birth what they spent a lifetime expecting. This is the reward of being a spiritual pioneer.

Jesus tells us Abraham experienced what Hebrews 11 and 12:1 promises. John 8:56 says: "Your father Abraham rejoiced to see My day, and he saw it and was glad." Jesus endured the cross for the joy set before Him, as Abraham endured in the same manner. Since Abraham spent a lifetime expecting but never seeing the fulfillment, God gave it to him by dream, vision and peering over the balconies of heaven as Jesus walked it out. Can you imagine Jeremiah and Isaiah cheering us on, rejoicing at our individual and corporate choices to embrace what they saw and prophesied?

We have the ability to make God rejoice if, like Abraham, we choose to embrace the full spectrum of prophetic preparation. As we interact and commit to growing the body, God desires development and depth in our choices, releasing the "…measure of the stature of fullness of Christ" (Ephesians 4:13). People should be healed and delivered not only in our churches, but everywhere we go, just like they were in Jesus' ministry. If doing what Jesus did is not consistently occurring where we fellowship, then we must embrace the promise and seek God to once again birth this anointing. God is faithful to restore what has been lost if we will choose to follow His path and plan.

The Marks That Identify Satan's Access

For nearly a century, the whole issue of receiving a mark has been clouded by prophetic teachers. Many have emphasized what Satan does versus viewing what God does through the "glorious victorious" church. Instead of majoring on the true marks of Christ, many leaders have taught and sensationalized the counterfeit mark (666) of the enemy. A sad fact of current Christianity is most believers know more about Satan's single counterfeit mark than they do about the real ones Jesus applies. Do we know how to recognize the counterfeit from the true? How can we have nearly an entire generation familiar with where Satan applies his most prominent seal, but have difficulty explaining the incremental steps that lead people to accept its application? God promises to "mark us" so that we can survive an end-time onslaught of pure evil. Will the "cost-less, cross-less, bless-me club" of American Christianity cry out for God's marks? Will we grow to discern the difference? Will we possess the spiritual authority necessary to harvest nations?

The phrase "marked men" usually conjures up an image from Revelation 13:11-18.

> *Then I saw another beast coming up out of the earth, and he had two horns like a lamb and spoke like a dragon. And he exercises all the authority of the first beast in his presence, and causes the earth and those who dwell in it to worship the first beast, whose deadly wound was healed. He performs great signs, so that he even makes fire come down from heaven on the earth in the sight of men.*

And he deceives those who dwell on the earth by those signs he has granted to do in the sight of the beast, telling those who dwell on the earth to make an image to the beast who was wounded by the sword and lived. He was granted power to give breath to the image of the beast, that the image of the beast should both speak and cause as many as would not worship the image of the beast to be killed. And he causes all, both small and great, rich and poor, free and slave, to receive a mark on their right hand or on their foreheads, and that no one may buy or sell except one who has the mark or the name of the beast, or the number of his name. Here is wisdom. Let him who has understanding calculate the number of the beast, for it is the number of a man: His number is 666.

The very first end-time book I remember reading nearly 35 years ago was entitled *666*. Throughout the twentieth century, many "last days" ministries have played upon the sincere desire of the church to know how to prepare for the future. A flood of speculative information based on European and Middle Eastern current events has assaulted, inoculated and anesthetized the church. The popular *Left Behind* series has raised the prominence of the entire issue of being marked. If we are to discern the full measure of our gifting and calling, now is the time to pray like Solomon, for the **shaw-maw** of God.

"Now, O LORD my God, You have made Your servant king instead of my father David, but I am a little child; I do not know how to go out or come in. And Your servant is in the midst of Your people whom You have chosen, a great people, too numerous to be numbered or counted. Therefore give to Your servant an understanding heart to judge Your people, that I may discern between good and evil. For who is able to judge this great people of Yours?"

The speech pleased the LORD, that Solomon had asked this thing. Then God said to him: "Because you have asked this thing, and have not asked long life for yourself, nor have asked riches for yourself, nor have asked the life of your enemies, but have asked for yourself understanding to discern justice, behold, I have done according to your words;

see, I have given you a wise and understanding heart, so that there has not been anyone like you before you, nor shall any like you arise after you. And I have also given you what you have not asked: both riches and honor, so that there shall not be anyone like you among the kings all your days. So if you walk in My ways, to keep My statutes and My commandments, as your father David walked, then I will lengthen your days."

1 Kings 3:7-14

Solomon asked for **shaw-maw**. It is both a panoramic and specific word used for a tongue or language. Solomon was asking God, "Speak to me in the language of my nativity that I may understand and perceive and act accordingly." The word **shaw-maw** includes the ability to separate, to make distinct, or to stand apart as one with the power of discerning, to know by the Spirit or to turn the mind and cause to understand. It also has within its concept basic intelligence or the ability to rationally debate and bring forth a skilled rebuttal against that which seems right, but is in fact, nefarious.

If we as the church were to seek God for His **shaw-mah**, surely an emphasis on the real mark would begin to thrive while interest in the pseudo would diminish. The amazing thing about the application of **shaw-mah** to the issue of 666 is that a clear choice emerges when applying God's Word to sweep away confusion. Would you rather spend time with the genuine article or with the counterfeit? Anyone who has seen television coverage of Middle Eastern Muslim protests has witnessed the fruit of Satan's mark—murderous hatred. Jesus identified the source in John 8:44 when He said:

You are of your father the devil, and the desires of your father you want to do. He was a murderer from the beginning, and does not stand in the truth, because there is no truth in him. When he speaks a lie, he speaks from his own resources, for he is a liar and the father of it.

If you ever wondered how Satan marks his people, just view the demonic hatred manifested on Islamic faces at the mention of America or Israel. Demonized Imams spread their hatred to congregations until both subjugated women and children are willing to blow themselves up just to kill us. Jesus paid the price for a harvest of Muslims. Can the church gain that harvest without moving God's hand of judgment on the radicals? The freedom of religion our forefathers died for did not include the murderous Islamic doctrine of demons. No free nation can tolerate radical Islam and stay free! The choice is ours.

> *Then I saw another angel ascending from the east, having the SEAL of the living God. And he cried with a loud voice to the four angels to whom it was granted to harm the earth and the sea, saying, "Do not harm the earth, the sea, or the trees till we have SEALED the servants of our God on their foreheads."*
>
> Revelation 7:2-3

Judgment only begins after the last believer is sealed. Why have we had to endure a century of ministry focusing on the counterfeit, when we clearly should have been embracing the real? As the church approaches the culmination of the ages, ever-greater confrontations emerge between forces of light and darkness.

> *He that is unjust, let him be unjust still: and he which is filthy let him be filthy still: and he that is righteous, let him be righteous still: and he that is holy, let him be holy still.*
>
> Revelation 22:11 (KJV)

The *Weymouth* translation defines the Greek word for "still"[1] as portraying an ever-increasing development and crystallization of character for the final confrontations between the devil and the church, manifesting the full nature of the God to which each group adheres. The church should fully represent Jesus in character, thought, word and deed (fullness) while those who refuse the Lord will act exactly like the devil (fullness). Who can forget the demonized Islamists taking heads off innocent people? When a nation stupidly extends freedom to the treasonous, they invite destruction. The warfare is between spirit and soul, even in the church.

> *But know this, that in the last days perilous times will come: for men will be lovers of themselves, lovers of money, boasters, proud, blasphemers, disobedient to parents,*

unthankful, unholy, unloving, unforgiving, slanderers, without self-control, brutal, despisers of good, traitors, headstrong, haughty, lovers of pleasure rather than lovers of God, having a form of godliness but denying its power. And from such people turn away! For of this sort are those who creep into households and made captives of gullible women loaded down with sins, led away by various lusts, always learning and never able to come to the knowledge of the truth. Now as Jannes and Jambres resisted Moses, so do these also resist the truth: men of corrupt minds, disapproved concerning the faith; but they will progress no further, for their folly will be manifest to all, as theirs also was.

2 Timothy 3:1-9

The issue of "...having a form of godliness but denying the power thereof..." is becoming a problem for both the Evangelical and Pentecostal/Charismatic streams of the church. On the Evangelical side, some leaders teach and strongly encourage people to be suspicious of anyone who prays in tongues or exercises any of the nine gifts of the Spirit. On the other side of this issue, some in the Pentecostal/Charismatic stream are resistant to the application of the cross which emphasizes humility and Christlike character development through adversity. Both streams have a serious segment of the truth.

Jesus cannot be thrilled with the doctrinal divisions of His body. Rome is burning while the church is fiddling! In verses 6-9 of 2 Timothy 3, we should be encouraged by the promise; God has set a boundary for evil and rebellion. Just as Jannes and Jambres could only counterfeit the power of God to a point, so it will be in the last days. The enemy can only counterfeit God's working in His church to a point. In the process of Antichrist rising, everything he does is to copy what the real has already established.

Ask yourself this: Why does the Antichrist have to perform signs, wonders and miracles? The logical answer in harmony with the church's activities in Acts is that the biblical mark has already been applied. Church history records that additional generations of believers have risen to the same standard. What will church history record of our generation? God authenticated Jesus through signs, wonders and miracles, according to Acts 2:22. Satan must duplicate the power gifts for his emissaries to be authenticated, marked and accepted. God longs for the church in each generation to set the standard proclaimed by the Bible. In verse 9 of 2 Timothy 3, the scripture says, "...but they will progress no further, for their folly will be manifest to all, as theirs also was." We have an appointed season during the end-time harvest in which resistance will seem as a light affliction in comparison to what God is doing through the church. The glorious church is a biblical vision we must embrace, believe for and pursue! For the promise is sure. If we were to be raptured soon, would we forfeit any dramatic manifestations of God's prophetic promises? Has Psalm 2 been fulfilled?

> *I will declare the decree: The LORD has said to me, "You are My Son, Today I have begotten You. Ask of Me, and I will give You The nations for Your inheritance, and the ends of the earth for Your possession. You shall break them with a rod of iron; You shall dash them in pieces like a potter's vessel."*
>
> *Psalm 2:7-9*

Jesus bought and paid for an international ingathering! God is committed to a harvest of nations. Are we willing to pay the preparational price tag? I believe in the rapture! 1 Thessalonians 4:17 says we will have one. The question is, in which generation? Have we experienced the prophetic declarations of Amos?

> *On that day I will raise up The tabernacle of David, which has fallen down, And repair its damages; I will raise up its ruins And rebuild it as in the days of old; that they may possess the remnant of Edom, And all the Gentiles who are called by My name," says the LORD who does this thing. "Behold, the days are coming," says the LORD. "When the plowman shall overtake the reaper, and the treader of grapes him who sows seed; the mountains shall drip with sweet wine, and all the hills shall flow with it."*
>
> *Amos 9:11-13*

Press on toward the prize

Run toward the call,

That God's fullness and glory

Upon us will fall.

At the season appointed

My Church will unfold,

In pureness and power

For the world to behold.

CHAPTER 2

Satan's Mammon Mark

Did I commit sin in abasing myself that you might be exalted, because I preached the gospel of God to you free of charge? I robbed other churches, taking wages from them to minister to you. And when I was present with you, and in need, I was a burden to no one, for what was lacking to me the brethren who came from Macedonia supplied. And in everything I kept myself from being burdensome to you, and so I will keep myself. As the truth of Christ is in me, no one shall stop me from this boasting in the regions of Achaia. Why? Because I do not love you? God knows!

But what I do, I will also continue to do, that I may cut off the opportunity from those who desire an opportunity to be regarded just as we are in the things of which they boast. For such are false apostles, deceitful workers, transforming themselves into apostles of Christ. And no wonder! For Satan himself transforms himself into an angel of light. Therefore it is no great thing if his ministers also transform themselves into ministers of righteousness, whose end will be according to their works.

2 Corinthians 11:7-15

Paul expressed a father's concern for the care and nurture of children. He determined to establish a ministerial standard handing each congregation a yardstick by which to measure commitment, credibility and servanthood. Paul seems to draw the distinction out of the life he has led before the Father in apostolic ministry. He says the mark of true apostolic ministry was apparent by the absence of a spirit of mammon. The path to such a place usually involved great crucifixion. True apostles can minister without demanding financial guarantees, first class travel, accommodations and all expenses paid. Only the real ministry could afford to offer everything God gave them without manipulation and self-promotion. He seems to suggest the mammon-motivated counterfeits are incapable of choosing such a path. The pseudo apparently have no guarantee God will provide for them, therefore, they have to carve out a niche through personal promotion.

On the other hand, Paul says committing to the divine standard releases a heavenly grace to totally abandon self to God by refusing to manipulate for money, knowing the Lord will provide. Jesus made everything available to the church without cost and without price. Paul chose this path for a specific reason. God wants the church established in purity. Paul apparently makes this choice based on the foundational importance of the apostolic office. He seems to be saying that he is making a personal choice in verse 12:

> *But what I do, I will also continue to do, that I may cut off the opportunity from those who desire an opportunity to be regarded just as we are in the things of which they boast.*

Paul makes a personal decision to establish a yardstick whereby the church can measure the difference between the counterfeit and the real. He does not demand that all other ministries live by his yardstick, but he chooses to "raise the bar." This was an issue that apparently became a mark in his generation for distinguishing the difference between those who claimed to be apostles and those who really were. Can we expect God to restore the same level of apostolic anointing if we are not willing to commit to the same standard?

In 2 Corinthians 12:14-18, Paul speaks again to this issue:

> *Now for the third time I am ready to come to you. And I will not be burdensome to you; for I do not seek yours, but you. For the children ought not to lay up for the parents, but the parents for the children. And I will very gladly spend*

and be spent for your souls; though the more abundantly I love you, the less I am loved. But be that as it may, I did not burden you. Nevertheless, being crafty, I caught you with guile! Did I take advantage of you by any of those whom I sent to you? I urged Titus, and sent our brother with him. Did Titus take advantage of you? Did we not walk in the same spirit? Did we not walk in the same steps?

Paul is demonstrating the true apostolic heart, one of servanthood. He was compelled to serve the church. Because God sent him, God obligated Himself to support the work. He will spread the visionary revelational table as a true servant of Jesus Christ, without cost. In Paul's mind, only the true can conduct business in such a manner. He also says in verses 17 and 18 that all those he trained walked in the same spirit. He demanded they walk in the same steps. Certain financial practices such as selling a mailing list would have been unthinkable to Paul. Recruiting churches to sign up under his apostolic covering for a percentage of income would have undoubtedly brought a scathing judgment, parallel to what Peter pronounced on Simon in Acts 8:20-22. Weymouth "parts the waters" with his comments, "…Find out by prayer whether, the offense being so rank and therefore the possibility of pardon so doubtful, the sin can nevertheless be forgiven."[2]

One of my adjunct professors in seminary made a point of emphatically telling us, "God created the nations while man created denominations. God's vision has no fences." This mentor paid a price to follow where the Spirit bade him go because his denomination rescinded his ordination for taking the power of the Holy Spirit to Rome. God ultimately vindicated his obedience by giving him the international nickname, "Mr. Pentecost." True apostles have the whole church in their heart and should carefully consider limitations by labels and fences! Can we expect God to fully restore the five-fold ministry with its operation, anointing and function for the sake of the church? The answer to that has to be a clear resounding "Yes we can expect it!"

But there were also false prophets among the people, even as there will be false teachers among you, who will secretly bring in destructive heresies, even denying the LORD who bought them, and bring on themselves swift destruction. And many will follow their destructive ways, because of whom the way of truth will be blasphemed. By covetousness they will exploit you with deceptive words; for a long time their judgment has not been idle, and their destruction does not slumber. For if God did not spare the angels who sinned, but cast them down to hell and delivered them into chains of darkness, to be reserved for judgment; and did not spare the ancient world, but saved Noah, one of eight people, a preacher of righteousness, bringing in the flood on the world of the ungodly; and turning the cities of Sodom and Gomorrah into ashes, condemned them to destruction, making them an example to those who afterward would live ungodly; and delivered righteous Lot, who was oppressed with the filthy conduct of the wicked (for that righteous man, dwelling among them, tormented his righteous soul from day to day by seeing and hearing their lawless deeds) —then the LORD knows how to deliver the godly out of temptations and to reserve the unjust under punishment for the day of judgment,....

2 Peter 2:1-9

Mammon Makes God Mad

Paul was not the only one who believed the greatest enemy of the true was a spirit of mammon. Peter was present when Jesus punctuated His ministry in the beginning (John 2) and at the end (Mark 11) with the rage of the Temple cleansing! Peter never forgot it. The two house cleanings in the Temple marked Peter for life. Watching the God Who created the universe rip apart the Jewish "swap meet" in an unparalleled outburst left everyone speechless. The only scripture they could think of to even remotely describe what they experienced was, "Zeal for Your house has eaten Me up" (Psalm 69:9). What Jesus did spiritually in the "Temple bazaars" must have made Arnold's performance in "The Terminator" movie look tame! Seeing that Peter was present, we should not be surprised in Acts 8 that he doubts if Simon can even obtain forgiveness, because the sin of attempting to buy God's blessing is so grievous. If buying it is grievous for a new believer, how much worse is it for a leader to manipulate, promote and profit from it? As God continues to restore the full measure of His anointing through the five-fold ministry, with a goal of releasing the church into the "full measure of the stature of Christ," we should expect outpourings of zeal to eat ministers up when confronting the spirit of mammon.

Peter demonstrates the same standard, as Paul, by commenting on individuals who apparently do not have the grace to deny themselves in order to bless others (this is a core concept of Christ). These false ministries apparently rejected or were never empowered with the grace to embrace the cross. Personal sacrifice for the sake of the body is the pattern of the cross. They appear incapable of walking this apostolic path. Peter says in 2 Peter 2:3 (KJV), "And through covetousness shall they with feigned words make merchandise of you:…" (see *Purifying the Altar*). Can you hear the zeal in that statement? Jesus was not the only one to be baptized in zeal.

The Greek word translated here "merchandise" is **em-por-ee-yoo-sawn-tai** meaning "to travel as a merchant, to travel on business, to carry on business, to set up a market, to cheat, to make a gain of or to exploit."[3] Many of us have probably participated in meetings where this spirit was present. We have been at conferences where an equal amount of time was given to advertising and selling material as was given to ministry. When the spirits of manipulation and mammon are present, the Holy Spirit is grieved and witnesses accordingly. If we have experienced this and it has made us angry, we are in good company. Jesus could not stomach the manifestation of this spirit and reacted dramatically when exposed. He was spiritually compelled to confront, castigate and cauterize this cancer. A sad comment on the condition of today's ministry is how readily accepted these previously forbidden practices have become! The early church did not conquer the Roman Empire by yielding to mammon.

The depth of the mammon infestation of the priesthood was so serious as to spark Jesus' most dramatic ministerial response; like an exterminator chasing cockroaches, He applies the only spiritual pesticide available. Alfred Edersheim who wrote about this period in the "Life and Times of Jesus the Messiah" said, "Herod went through four priestly families until he found one that would do all his will (Caiaphas)."

> *Now the Passover of the Jews was at hand, and Jesus went up to Jerusalem. And He found in the temple those who sold oxen and sheep and doves, and the moneychangers doing business. When He had made a whip of cords, He drove them all out of the temple, with the sheep and the oxen, and poured out the changers' money and overturned the tables. And He said to those who sold doves, "Take these things away! Do not make My Father's house a house of merchandise!" Then His disciples remembered that it was written, "Zeal for Your house has eaten Me up."*
>
> John 2:13-17

The Greek word **em-por-ee-on** conveys the very antithesis of what God blesses. In Peter's second epistle, covetousness is the motivation for developing an **em-por-ee-on**. Men who yield to mammon make ministry merchandise marts for money. In three and a half years with Jesus, the only thing that triggered divine wrath of this magnitude was mammon. Jesus' reaction to mammon was so shocking to all present that the disciples were duly impressed with a life-lesson. Peter acted like he never forgot it. Paul must have received it by revelation.

Once we succumb to the spirit of mammon, three principles weave their deadly web around us and gain preeminence: packaging, promotion and profit. Peter and Paul were in full harmony concerning what separates the counterfeit from the true. They both applied the same yardstick. They measured ministry by the mammon test. Those who fail this test are on the path of receiving Satan's mark. They are doing their own thing. On the other hand, those who pass this test usually have the marks of the cross to prove it.

Have you been empowered

To embrace the cross?

With Paul will you gain Christ

Counting all things as loss?

With pure, humble heart

Do you seek servanthood?

Know promotion and profit

Yields stubble and wood!

CHAPTER 3

Mammon's Mistress

No one can serve two masters; for either he will hate the one and love the other, or else he will be loyal to the one and despise the other. You cannot serve God and mammon.

Matthew 6:24

Perhaps there is a reason why the mark of the true and the mark of the counterfeit seem to center around the issue of money. If we look at the phony mark we have heard so much about for decades, we can possibly discover why the central focus seems to revolve around the issue of mammon.

And he causes all, both small and great, rich and poor, free and slave, to receive a mark on their right hand or on their foreheads, and that no one may buy or sell except one who has the mark or the name of the beast, or the number of his name.

Revelation 13:16-17

The foundation of the counterfeit mark is mammon: no one can "buy or sell without it." If you cannot "buy or sell," then you can no longer earn what is necessary to live. You can no longer provide essentials for your family. The counterfeit mark ultimately becomes an issue of life or death. Since the counterfeit is a life or death choice physically, we can deduce that the true mark reflects a life or death choice spiritually. We must ask ourselves, what is the enemy trying to duplicate? What is he trying to copy? What is the root issue? What purpose is he pursuing? The answer is control. When people consistently refuse to yield spiritually, they must be forced physically.[4] Is the true mark an issue of control or a mark of personal choice and submission? When the enemy institutes the counterfeit mark, he works in the area of the flesh and his control mechanism forces a choice: starve or bow in worship by receiving his mark. Mammon temptations increasingly demonstrate, by the choices we make, the God which we serve.

In over three decades of traveling ministry, the majority of church leaders I have encountered have been exceptionally upstanding, honest and God-fearing individuals. A number of years ago, I was doing a conference with several well-known ministers. The pastor shared the amount of the honorarium he was paying the primary speaker, but never sent the check. About three months later, inadvertently this same speaker discovered in a conversation with the business manager that the pastor had taken the honorarium and put a new motor in his own vehicle. The pastor made a choice that day which made him mammon's mistress. He committed financial fornication.

Several months later, on behalf of my ministry cohort, I confronted the pastor and he repented. I had hoped for his sake the issue was resolved, even though he had made no restitution. Later, I was told of an African missionary who spent a week ministering in this church and the pastor treated him the same way—that missionary did a week's work with no remuneration. Financial fornication is a fact of life, but once a person chooses to become mammon's mistress, extricating himself can be terribly difficult. His spirit becomes impregnated with defiling seed. That pastor, had he been faithful to his covenant with God, should be reaching the apex of his calling, but is no longer in ministry. The fastest way I know to forfeit your gifting, calling and even your life is choosing financial fornication and becoming "mammon's mistress." *DON'T DO IT—IF YOU WANT TO LIVE!*

We must discern and confront financial fornication wherever we encounter it. A recent SOS e-mail received in our office explains the extensive nature of the current mammon crisis in the church. The son of an 80-year-old widow wrote:

"I am rather melancholy now because a few months ago my mom called me very upset that her pastor wrote her a letter asking for a pledge of $100,000. She could not see how they could do that to an 80-year-old widow. So I wrote my friends with an SOS who used to go there to try to bring this to a halt. I used a number of scriptures in the OT and NT.... Then I received a blistering letter back from them telling me that I am full of rage, anger and bitterness toward the church, and foaming Bible verses from the mouth like a rabid dog. Well, this blew me away because they had been good Christian friends for 20 years. They were very happy at that church. But I had to defend my mom and her interests. Well, now I have lost two more friends. But this is nothing new. Keeping friends, now that is something new."

Is the church obligated to help take care of widows or pillage and plunder them? When we choose to confront mammon and take a stand for righteousness, a serious price tag emerges. 2 Timothy 2:19 says, "Nevertheless the solid foundation of God stands, having this seal: 'The Lord knows those who are His,' and, 'Let everyone who names the name of Christ depart from iniquity." The absence of mammon becomes a mark or seal upon the true believer as we embrace the standard of biblical purity and choose to walk accordingly. Ephesians promises a church without spot, wrinkle or blemish. God is looking for those who are willing to pay the price and show the way. The same zeal that God demonstrated through Jesus may come upon some members of the church.

Merging Evangelical and Charismatic Criteria

In Acts 2:22, we find another mark the Father gives to the Son. Verse 22 says:

Men of Israel, hear these words: Jesus of Nazareth, a Man attested by God to you by miracles, wonders, and signs which God did through Him in your midst, as you yourselves also know—....

What was God's mark of approval on the Son? What was His attestation to the authenticity of the ministry of Jesus? Did God issue a stamp like "USDA Approved" or "UL Approved?" He did! And we are told exactly what that seal/stamp/approval was. God's mark of approval, attestation and authenticity was "miracles, wonders, and signs which God did through Him." Acts 2:22 identifies a distinct mark of God that was on Jesus. This same mark is supposed to authenticate the church. In the last days, it is obviously so effective, it must be counterfeited.

> *Now, brethren, concerning the coming of our Lord Jesus Christ and our gathering together to Him, we ask you, not to be soon shaken in mind or troubled, either by spirit or by word or by letter, as if from us, as though the day of Christ had come. Let no one deceive you by any means;* **for that Day will not come** *unless the falling away comes first, and the man of sin is revealed, the son of perdition, who opposes and exalts himself above all that is called God or that is worshiped, so that he sits as God in the temple of God, showing himself that he is God. Do you not remember that when I was still with you I told you these things? And now you know what is restraining, that he may be revealed in his own time. For the mystery of lawlessness is already at work; only He who now restrains* **will do so** *until He is taken out of the way. And then the* **lawless** *one will be revealed, whom the Lord will consume with the breath of His mouth and destroy with the brightness of His coming. The coming of the lawless one is according to the working of Satan, with all power, signs, and lying wonders, and with all unrighteousness deception among those who perish, because they did not receive the love of the truth, that they might be saved. And for this reason God will send them strong delusion, that they should believe the lie, that they all may be condemned who did not believe the truth but had pleasure in unrighteousness.*
>
> *2 Thessalonians 2:1-12*

Segments of the church have used this passage to scare and corral their parishioners, keeping them from participating in various phases of Spirit-led restoration. While many in leadership herald the imminent rapture of the church, they have unknowingly hindered it by isolating their people. They have warned their congregations about ministers who follow the Spirit as deceived and untrustworthy, when that label could also be appropriately descriptive of them. Fencing in the sheep for the sole reason of preserving budgets is a form of financial fornication. Mammon is a very adept deceiver.

In the first place, the people described in 2 Thessalonians 2 are only led astray "...because they did not receive the knowledge/love of the truth..." and accept Jesus as Lord. The lying signs and wonders only work among the rebellious, who by choice, wander out of God's protective custody (covenant relationship) because God sends **strong delusion**. This passage clearly suggests that the true and real have blazed such a trail of signs, wonders, and miracles resulting in an end-time harvest, that the only way the enemy has any opportunity of performing his chief purpose is to identify with the stream of miraculous signs common in the church in order to gain equal acceptance.

Ezekiel 28 and Isaiah 14 reveal the nature of the enemy which we will see in the last days. Those descriptions come from the fall, when prophets spoke concerning how Satan became the enemy of God, and why he was kicked out of heaven. We are told in Ezekiel 28:14 that he was "...the anointed cherub who covers..."—he was in the garden of God—he was perfect in the day he was created. Within his body were the instruments to make music and apparently lead the angels in holy worship. Isaiah 14 records the sin that was found in him. Verses 12-14 state:

> *How you are fallen from heaven, O Lucifer, son of the morning! How you are cut down to the ground, You who weakened the nations! For you have said in your heart; "I **will** ascend into heaven, I **will** exalt my throne above the stars of God; I **will** also sit on the mount of the congregation On the farthest sides of the north; I **will** ascend above the heights of the clouds, I **will** be like the Most High." Yet you shall be brought down to Sheol, To the lowest depths of the Pit.*

The five "I wills" of Isaiah 14 not only reveal character, but indicate behavior. It is obvious from these declarations why Satan must act as described in 2 Thessalonians 2. Isaiah 14 says:

> "I *will* ascend into heaven, I *will* exalt my throne above the stars of God, I *will* sit on the mount of the congregation… I *will* ascend above the heights of the clouds, I *will* be like the Most High."

Is it any wonder in 2 Thessalonians chapter 2 we read he must prove to "…himself that he is God." This description of Satan shows us why he will operate in the manner described. He must oppose and exalt himself above all that is called God or that is worshiped. He must do that in order to prove to himself that he is God. The emerging warfare against the church will bring life or death choices. Are we preparing the next generation to face these choices? How can we lead others to God's mark if we do not have it ourselves? Do we recognize the counterfeit marks of the enemy? 2 Thessalonians warns us Satan will copy what the church is doing "…with all power signs and lying wonders…." Revelation 13 also reveals warnings which must be heeded by Pentecostal and Charismatic churches. This demands that "Spirit-filled" congregations no longer automatically accept all who exercise signs and wonders just because of the miraculous. **Evangelical churches are right to demand character and integrity.** The season may be fast approaching when we can no longer bless all those who move in the "power of the spirit," especially if they lack God's thumbprint. Jeremiah was grieved by the prophets who prophesied by Baal and we should be grieved by the prophets who prophesy by mammon. We must see if the Bible adds some additional marks insuring our acceptance of true ministry.

The Real Precedes the Counterfeit

> Then I saw another beast coming up out of the earth, and he had two horns like a lamb and spoke like a dragon. And he exercises all the authority of the first beast in his presence, and causes the earth and those who dwell in it to worship the first beast, whose deadly wound was healed. He performs

great signs, so that he even makes fire come down from heaven on the earth in the sight of men.

Revelation 13:11-13

Many in the church seem to be getting excited about the restoration of all the Ephesians chapter 4 five-fold ministry giftings. Yet they have not been restored to the point where they are calling fire down from heaven or announcing Ananias and Sapphiras, restoring the *"fear of the Lord."* We know such a season is approaching because the book of Revelation depicts a time when the counterfeit are copying the real! Verse 14 says:

And he deceives those who dwell on the earth by those signs which he was granted to do in the sight of the beast, telling those who dwell on the earth to make an image to the beast who was wounded by the sword and lived.

Verse 15 says:

He was granted power to give breath to the image of the beast, that the image of the beast should both speak and cause as many as would not worship the image of the beast to be killed.

Those who saw and were present for the performance of these signs and wonders believed and then yielded to the will of the counterfeit. Satan was apparently successful in destroying those who did not receive him. A theology preparing people for Antichrist is probably being taught in your neighborhood—it is Islam. Persecution is coming. I know this much—God commanded me to prepare His people! Those who said "no" to Satan, "Your miracles are not God," those with discernment and those who could tell the difference between the counterfeit and the real chose not to worship and paid the ultimate price. As Christians, they were present and forced to make a choice. Even if we believe in a pre-tribulation rapture, we must admit thousands of believers are martyred yearly. The primary force killing Christians and Jews is Islam. The thousands that die every year giving the ultimate witness as seed sown for a greater harvest have not taken God by surprise.

The attitude of the North American churches is, "It won't happen here." **Hear** the prophetic word of the Lord: If it cannot happen here, why did God command me to prepare His people? *Now is a time of grace to prepare.* In over 30 years of ministry, it seems the church only prepares for what it believes. If we believe in rapture, that is all we prepare to face, but the rapture does not preclude persecution. It is quite probable to have a rapture preceded by intense seasons of persecution. Wouldn't it be wise to prepare now? Preparation now will yield peace then. It is the only wise thing to do.

Satan seems compelled to counterfeit the resurrection. If the counterfeiter feels he is forced to emulate the resurrection, then raising the dead must be prominent in the church during this season. We should expect the church to be resurrecting people as the fruit of following the Acts 1-5 pattern (see "In One Accord" CD series). The church will replace body parts, proving the Creator lives. Believers apparently will be doing such dramatic signs and wonders that the judgment of God comes on the world for not receiving the true. This judgment releases a delusion which enables acceptance of the counterfeit. It is only after rejecting the true performance of signs and wonders that people believe the counterfeit. They become thoroughly incarcerated in deception, accepting a false mark on the right hand or the forehead as a sign of worship.

We should consider the reality of the church walking in resurrection power, growing out arms and legs to the degree it must be counterfeited by the enemy in order for his servants to achieve credibility. Why major on what the enemy does, when it actually points us toward a glorious, victorious church? God's definition of "glorious-victorious" is seen in the overcoming of all obstacles of the early church as they fought to impact the then known world.

The same temptation Jesus faced in Luke 4:5-8 becomes the foundation for Satan's mark.

> *And he causes all, both small and great, rich and poor, free and slave, to receive a mark on their right hand or on their foreheads, and that no one may buy or sell except one who has the mark or the name of the beast, or the number of his name.*
>
> *Revelation 13:16-17*

The "buy or sell" issue becomes a foundation for understanding the purpose of the mark as we progress through the book of Revelation and see the connection. Revelation 14, verses 9 and 10 give us a key:

> *Then a third angel followed them, saying with a loud voice, "If anyone worships the beast and his image, and receives his mark on his forehead or on his hand, he himself shall also drink of the wine of the wrath of God, which is poured out full strength into the cup of His indignation. And he shall be tormented with fire and brimstone in the presence of the holy angels and in the presence of the Lamb."*

Verse 11 accentuates the connection between the mark and worship. It says:

> *And the smoke of their torment ascends forever and ever; and they have no rest day or night, who worship the beast and his image, and whoever receives the mark of his name.*

Who Will We Worship?

Bowing to mammon is a spiritual preparation for accepting the counterfeit mark. Those who yield to mammon now will be conditioned to accept Satan's mark later. Bowing to mammon and receiving the mark = worship! The theme of the book of Revelation is **who will we worship,** as freedom progressively disintegrates and governments control their people! Revelation 15 makes it very clear there are people throughout this period who refuse to worship the Antichrist. Verse 2 says:

> *And I saw something like a sea of glass mingled with fire, and those who have the **victory** over the beast, over his image and over his mark and over the number of his name, standing on the sea of glass, having harps of God.*

There are those who choose not to bow or yield, refusing financial fornication. In Revelation 16:2 once again, we find taking the mark is worshiping Antichrist. Verse 2 says:

> *So the first went and poured out his bowl upon the earth, and a foul and loathsome sore came upon the men who had the **mark** of the beast and those who **worshiped** his image.*

We are beginning to see that accepting the enemy's mark is bowing, yielding, submitting or acknowledging Antichrist, thus extending worship. Yielding to mammon's temptations gives Satan worship. Revelation 19:20 says:

> *Then the beast was captured, and with him the false prophet who worked signs in his presence, by which he deceived those who received the mark of the beast and those who* **worshiped** *his image. These two were cast alive into the lake of fire burning with brimstone.*

Now in chapter 20, verse 4, we see God speaking specifically to those who refused to worship the counterfeit. Verse 4 says:

> *And I saw thrones, and they sat on them, and judgment was committed to them. And I saw the souls of those who had been beheaded for their witness to Jesus and for the word of God, who had* **not worshiped** *the beast or his image, and had not received his mark on their foreheads or on their hands. And they lived and reigned with Christ for a thousand years.*

What theology today encourages its followers to behead Christians and Jews? Perhaps the church needs to realize World War III has been declared and is being fought by everyone but us—the chief target. The only people as demonically deluded as Islamists are those politicians who believe we can negotiate with them. The antiwar peaceniks of previous generations have become deluded leaders willing to negotiate freedom away by utter inactivity. God demands a harvest from Islam and we must prepare to get it!

A single thread traverses Revelation: **whom will we worship?** The early chapters of Revelation all describe scenes of visible worship by apostles, elders and angels. Chapter 4 is full of descriptive language concerning living creatures worshiping and giving glory, followed by twenty-four elders who worship. In chapter 5, we see the Lamb, who has qualified to take the Book and open it because He **worshiped** with self-sacrifice. He worshiped God and was willing to embrace the cross, establishing a pattern. Revelation 5 portrays every living creature in heaven, on earth and under the earth **worshiping** God, bowing before Him and saying:

> *Blessing and honor and glory and power Be to Him who*
> *sits on the throne, And to the Lamb, forever and ever!*

We see each chapter thus far full of worship, with chapter 6 transitioning to judgments. Chapter 7 describes God sealing or marking His believers.

> *After these things I saw four angels standing at the four*
> *corners of the earth, holding the four winds of the earth, that*
> *the wind should not blow on the earth, on the sea, or on any*
> *tree. Then I saw another angel ascending from the east,*
> *having the seal of the living God. And he cried with a loud*
> *voice to the four angels to whom it was granted to harm the*
> *earth and the sea, saying, "Do not harm the earth, the sea, or*
> *the trees till we have sealed the servants of our God on their*
> *foreheads."*
>
> Revelation 7:1-3

Usually, a safe way to approach the interpretation of complex books or passages like Revelation is to search for theme and thread. When the same thread appears consistently, it usually points us to the theme. The thread and theme is clear! **Fullness** of commitment becomes worship and is rewarded by a mark. Revelation's theme is: **Whom are we going to worship?** Two opposing groups are contrasted in Revelation with the same core commitment, manifested in worship and ultimately rewarded with a mark. Those who worship God receive His seal. Those who worship the devil receive his counterfeit mark. Whether we get the real or the counterfeit depends on whom we worship. This becomes the emerging thread which runs throughout Revelation. We now have to ask ourselves: If the dividing line is whom we *worship — God* or the counterfeit—how does chapter 13:16-17 ultimately impact this overall theme and what constitutes worship?

> *And he causes all, both small and great, rich and poor, free*
> *and slave, to receive a mark on their right hand or on their*
> *foreheads, and that no one may buy or sell except one who*
> *has the mark or the name of the beast, or the number of his*
> *name.*
>
> Revelation 13:16-17

Just as God is willing to sow into one generation as preparation for what He wants done in the next (David and Solomon), so the enemy is patient enough to make progressive corruption so commonplace and appealing that the prevailing attitude is not shock and revulsion but "So what, everybody does it."

The choices we make are visible in the actions we take, thus proving which God we serve. Worship is much more than 30 minutes of singing on Sunday morning. *Our worship is demonstrated by how we live our lives*—whether or not we adhere to God's Word. The degree to which Satan can lure us away from a life of spiritual integrity dictates the level at which he has stolen our worship. At this point in time, we should not be nearly so worried about the coming mark of Antichrist as we are about the worship we may already be giving, but just do not realize it!

The issues of Satanic worship and receiving his mark are initiated and enforced by the spirit of mammon. Jesus made it very clear—we "...**cannot** serve God and mammon." Satan brings to man the very essence of what he presented Jesus: "Worship me and you can have what you want." If spiritual warfare increasingly manifests in this dimension, then perhaps we should ask ourselves what the necessary steps are for equipping a generation to survive the battle and finish their race. In Luke 4, verses 5 and 6, the scripture says:

> *Then the devil, taking Him up on a high mountain, showed Him all the kingdoms of the world in a moment of time. And the devil said unto Him, "All this authority [ex-oo-see-ah] I will give You, and their glory; for this has been delivered to me, and I give it to whomever I wish."*

To receive the full measure of Holy Spirit power, we must face and pass mammon tests. Jesus was called to gain **ex-oo-see-ah** (authority) over all these kingdoms through the cross—through death, burial and resurrection. Satan offered Him a shortcut. This scene will one day be repeated as the counterfeit Christ offers individuals and nations his seal. How is the enemy readying people to accept his mark? Through deception—the same shortcuts often tempt us if we could only recognize them for what they are! When we violate integrity by making choices resulting in financial fornication, Satan trumpets it before God as worship received (see *Purifying the Altar* for in-depth application).[5] Verse 7 says:

Therefore, if You will worship before me, all will be Yours.

Satan seeks worship. How much will the church continue to provide? LIVE IN FINANCIAL INTEGRITY. DO NOT ALLOW YOUR WORSHIP TO BE STOLEN!

A sure sign of integrity

Is what you do financially.

Will you pass

The "mammon test"?

Your heart forged pure…

The goal—God's best!

CHAPTER 4

The Koo-ree-os Test

The Greek word for "master" in Matthew 6:24 is **koo-ree-os**, and ultimately means the one glorified by our actions. We make choices daily which reflect Lordship by glorifying one of two masters. Choices that honor God's Word and uphold personal integrity reflect true worship. Actions which violate personal integrity for financial gain reveal mammon worship, honor Satan and potentially end in eternal destruction.

Our preparational pattern will probably in some way parallel the Master's. Contributing aspects of the **koo-ree-os** test begin to unfold in Luke 16:1:

> And He also said to His disciples: "There was a certain rich man who had a steward, and an accusation was brought to him that this man was wasting his goods."

One small step of violating personal integrity for dishonest gain leads to many more steps in an ever-increasing pattern, resulting in real captivity. Over time, this can emerge as what seems like an unbreakable stronghold. The parable of the unjust steward has to be set in context. A red-letter Bible edition is very helpful for this purpose, because at first glance you notice Jesus has been speaking parables to the scribes and Pharisees answering their criticism of 15:2 concerning His ministry to sinners. After three parables explaining God's rejoicing when something that was lost (sheep, coin, son) is found, Jesus turns to His disciples in chapter 16 and speaks a parable about the prevailing spirit ruling the scribes and Pharisees who have spiritual stewardship over Israel.

Verses 2-8 state:

> *So he called him and said to him, "What is this I hear about you? Give an account of your stewardship, for you can no longer be steward." Then the steward said within himself, "What shall I do? For my master is taking the stewardship away from me. I cannot dig; I am ashamed to beg. I have resolved what to do, that when I am put out of the stewardship, they may receive me into their houses." So he called every one of his master's debtors to him, and said to the first, "How much do you owe my master?" And he said, "A hundred measures of oil." So he said to him, "Take your bill, and sit down quickly and write fifty." Then he said to another, "And how much do you owe?" So he said, "A hundred measures of wheat." And he said to him, "Take your bill, and write eighty." So the master commended the unjust steward because he had dealt shrewdly. For the sons of this world are more shrewd in their generation than the sons of light.*

Jesus congratulated the excellence of highly developed manipulation achieved by the priests, suggesting they had progressed much further in the spirit of mammon than honest believers had in the Spirit of God.

Verse 9 sarcastically warns:

> *And I say to you, make friends for yourself by unrighteous mammon, that when you fail, **they may receive** you into **everlasting habitations.***

Jesus was saying to His disciples in verse 9, "If you conduct your ministry like the 'scribes and Pharisees,' yielding to mammon at every opportunity, you will be sealing your eternal fate." The spirit of mammon brings captivity which has eternal consequences! The spirit of mammon and its cohorts ultimately have the assignment of preparing people to receive a counterfeit mark. The unjust steward used mammon and manipulation to gain man's favor while simultaneously forfeiting God's. Anyone who uses manipulation and mammon is guaranteed to fail the **koo-ree-os** test. Verses 10-14 of Luke 16 state:

> *He who is faithful in what is least is faithful also in much; and he who is unjust in what is least is unjust also in much. Therefore if you have not been faithful in the unrighteous mammon, who will commit to your trust the true riches? And if you have not been faithful in what is another man's, who will give you what is your own? No servant can serve two masters; for either he will hate the one and love the other, or else he will be loyal to the one and despise the other. You cannot serve God and mammon. Now the Pharisees, who were lovers of money, also heard all these things, and they derided Him.*

A personal mammon test can be as simple as whether or not to tithe or as complex as choosing to embrace a prophetic vision where the spiritual repercussions drag us into a Job-like adversity. The church has been encouraged to embrace God's prophetic promises of a "wealth transfer," not realizing the preparational price or the spiritual repercussions of such a move. Isaiah 61:6 and 7 states:

> *But you shall be named the Priests of the LORD, Men shall call you Servants of our God. You shall eat the riches of the Gentiles, And in their glory you shall boast. Instead of your shame you shall have double honor, And instead of confusion they shall rejoice in their portion. Therefore in their land they shall possess double; Everlasting joy shall be theirs.*

To embrace such a vision is to assault the very foundation of Satan's throne. It is possible to walk a straight and narrow line of biblical integrity while groaning inside due to the magnitude of personal warfare manifested in a lack of provision from attacking the enemy's largest stronghold. This seems to have been the pattern for many who embraced the "Anointing to Spoil"[6] only to discover this biblical vision becoming the main point of spiritual contention. To embrace a prophetic promise that attacks the very foundation of Satan's throne can eventually result in dissuading us from continuing because the personal price is so great! Sometimes a mammon-based

koo-ree-os test for ministry is whether or not we will preach the things which we know to be truth even if it costs us our biggest givers.

I am convinced ministers will face more Lordship tests than the average parishioner will. When we specifically preach only those things that profit us, we are using manipulation and have failed a mammon test. When we recruit and appoint, or attempt to elect, only those who have their own businesses or are wealthy, to our boards, we also violate the issue of integrity and fail the mammon test. Every time a special offering is taken, whether for building projects, traveling, overseas or specialized ministry, the failure to dispense funds according to the stated purpose constitutes a major integrity violation; and if personal gain is involved, it ultimately releases worship to the enemy.

It is painful to write about individuals I have known through the years who have consistently demanded sacrifice from their staff, missionaries, and traveling ministries who came through their churches, while they refused to sacrifice anything themselves. They would take the best of everything and give the least possible to staff and others. I have often thought, "God, how long will You allow this to continue?" When God stops those who repeatedly fail the **koo-ree-os** test—He may stop them permanently. I have seen pastors compromise financial integrity to gain a nest egg for retirement and suddenly, surprisingly, slam into God's zeal. In the end, they did not need retirement.

God can bring us to the end slowly or suddenly. No man can afford to consistently fail the **koo-ree-os** test and still expect to have the grace to finish his race. God led the early church to **fullness** of commitment through conquering mammon. Victoriously conquering mammon led to the double anointing. They went back to God, prayed, agreed on Psalm 2, and asked the Lord for a whole new level of authority. God answered their prayer. The second filling initiated a congregational **koo-ree-os** test. In Acts 4:32, we are told:

> *Now the multitude of those who believed were of one heart and one soul; neither did anyone say the any of the things he possessed was his own, but they had all things in common.*

The early church proved victorious over mammon by sowing into each other's needs. Barnabas, a Levite, passed the Lordship test. Ananias and Sapphira failed it. The rest is history! The Bible is full of individual and corporate mammon tests that God initiates and demands we walk through. We need to understand that this is not a minor issue. It is a major issue. It becomes the central thread in the book of Revelation, and those who fail the **koo-ree-os** test choose a course of action that will very likely end in demonic fullness and judgment. Yielding worship to mammon forfeits God's **fullness**.

It's a life or death issue

The mark that you wear.

Is the world's stamp upon you

Or the cross do you bear?

There's a "Lordship test" coming!

Saint, in order to shine

Is God's mark clearly on you

Saying, "This one is Mine"?

CHAPTER 5

How Should We Prepare?

Should we spend all of our time studying the rapture or should we allocate some resources to preparation for persecution? If our timing is errant about being "caught up," the failure to prepare for persecution could doom a generation. Did the early church have prophetic passages promising God would mark or seal them for the end-times? Amazingly enough, they did! We find the early church very specifically believed and preached God would seal them for what was coming because He was taking them through—not out! Their preparational passage was Ezekiel 9:1-7. It says:

> Then He called out in my hearing with a loud voice, saying, "Let those who have charge over the city draw near, each with a deadly weapon in his hand." And suddenly six men came from the direction of the upper gate, which faces north, each with his battle-ax in his hand. One man among them was clothed with linen and had a writer's inkhorn at his side. They went in and stood beside the bronze altar. Now the glory of the God of Israel had gone up from the cherub, where it had been, to the threshold of the temple. And He called to the man clothed with linen, who had the writer's inkhorn at his side; and the LORD said to him, "Go through the midst of the city, through the midst of Jerusalem, and put a mark on the foreheads of the men who sigh and cry over all the abominations that are done within it." To the others He said in my hearing, "Go after him through the city and kill; do

not let your eye spare, nor have any pity. Utterly slay old and young men, maidens and little children and women; but do not come near anyone on whom is the mark; and begin at My sanctuary." So they began with the elders who were before the temple. Then He said to them, "Defile the temple, and fill the courts with the slain. Go out!" And they went out and killed in the city.

The mark we see here has an appropriately rich etymological history and presents a very strong prophetic picture leading us toward understanding the qualification process. Judgment comes on the earth but starts in the church. Justice demands God mark the faithful and obedient before His judgment begins. Each blood-bought individual will be able to accomplish their divine assignments in victory even during an avalanche of judgment and death. Only those without God's mark are destroyed. The judgments, whether seals, trumpets or bowls, when poured out, bypass those who are marked. The Hebrew word translated "mark" in Ezekiel 9, according to the *Gesenius' Hebrew-Chaldee Lexicon,* was "a sign in the form of a cross branded on the thigh or neck of horses and camels, whence the name by the letter **tau** which in Phoenician, and on the coins of the Macabees has the form of the cross. From the Phoenicians, the Greeks and Romans took both the name and the form of the letter."[7]

The mark had a secondary meaning, "A mark subscribed instead of a name on a bill of complaint; *hence subscription…. It is stated at the Synod of Chalcedon and other Synods principally in the east, some even of the bishops being unable to write, put the sign of the cross instead of their names…."* So when the early church ministered to people about the end-times and judgments of God, they preached, "God seals the faithful" out of Ezekiel 9. The mark was obvious. It was the sign of the cross. When God marks His own, they bear the sign of the cross.

Ezekiel saw the righteous marked with the physical mark of the cross in a vision. This becomes the example of what we look for spiritually in the New Testament and therefore the dividing line between the counterfeit and the real. Those who embrace the application of the cross and walk in it will find themselves marked, fully empowered to hold their ground in the end-times. Those who refuse the cross will undoubtedly disqualify themselves, probably in a moment of extreme discouragement.

Perhaps a good place to begin looking at what it means to be marked with the cross is to examine the life of one who both experienced and wrote about it.

Identifying the Marks of God

In Acts 9:10-16, we get a glimpse of what God means when He talks about the application of the cross:

> *Now there was a certain disciple at Damascus named Ananias; and to him the Lord said in a vision, "Ananias." And he said, "Here I am, Lord." So the Lord said to him, "Arise and go to the street called Straight, and inquire at the house of Judas for one called Saul of Tarsus, for behold, he is praying. And in a vision he has seen a man named Ananias coming in and putting his hand on him, so that he might receive his sight." Then Ananias answered, "Lord, I have heard from many about this man, how much harm he has done to Your saints in Jerusalem. And here he has authority from the chief priests to bind all who call on Your name." But the Lord said to him, "Go, for he is a chosen vessel of Mine to bear My name before Gentiles, kings, and the children of Israel. For I will show him how many things he must **suffer** for **My name's sake**."*

Paul, at the very beginning of his ministry, in vision and by dramatic intervention, received a revelation of the price of walking out the will of the Father. The price involves **enduring adversity** that is supernatural, coming as a result of the call. We see it referred to many times often in different ways, but it always reflects the same theme. In Romans 8:15 and following we are told:

> *For you did not receive the spirit of bondage again to fear, but you received the Spirit of adoption by whom we cry out, "Abba, Father." The Spirit Himself bears witness with our spirit that we are children of God, and if children, then heirs—heirs of God and joint heirs with Christ, if indeed we **suffer with Him**, that we may also be glorified together.*

> *For I consider that the sufferings of this present time are not worthy to be compared with the glory which shall be revealed in us.*

Paul understood that walking in God's path would bring us into a conflict that carries a great measure of adversity and suffering. In that process, we would be living out the pattern Jesus experienced. Jesus lived a pattern which we are called to repeat. If we refuse to walk the path, then the part we play is limited, and we may reach a point where we can no longer speak accurately for God. In 1 Corinthians 4:4-5 Paul says:

> *For I know of nothing against myself, yet I am not justified by this; but He who judges me is the Lord. Therefore judge nothing before the time, until the Lord comes, who will both bring to light the hidden things of darkness and reveal the counsels of the hearts; and then each one's praise will come from God.*

Paul is demonstrating an attitude, which is consistently seen in the godly throughout scripture. One of the major signs reflecting application of the cross is the issue of humility. This is manifested in an individual's ability to accept or reject reproof. Proverbs says, "A wise man seeks reproof...." Paul is saying he invites the cross because he does not trust even himself; even if his conscience is clear, he still does not totally trust his heart. He is openly demonstrating the heart attitude of one who has embraced the cross. That constitutes a clear, distinct mark. It is the mark of humility, and it often only comes with being baptized in humiliation. The fruit of adversity is humility, compassion, and love. When adversity is applied, attitudes and thought-patterns change. The end result is that we become more like Jesus. In verses 6-8 of 1 Corinthians 4, Paul is dealing with the issue of personal choices for Christ's sake. Paul's counsel is clear—choose the cross and forgo the pride of attaining great spiritual knowledge. Verses 6-8 tell us:

> *Now these things, brethren, I have figuratively transferred to myself and Apollos for your sakes, that you may learn in us not to think beyond what is written, that none of you may be puffed up on behalf of one against the other. For who*

makes you differ from another? And what do you have that you did not receive? Now if you did indeed receive it, why do you glory as if you had not received it? You are already full! You are already rich! You have reigned as kings without us—and indeed I could wish you did reign, that we also might reign with you!

Paul is making it very clear that the Holy Spirit's gifts without the manifestation of the cross can open us up to pride, selfish ambition, and personal kingdom building. This climate often produces great self-promotion. It is rampant in our day and time. Madison Avenue marketing techniques seem to rule ministry more often than the humility we see displayed here. Following such a course is very dangerous because an anointing elevates, while the refusal to apply the cross forces us to sow and harvest mixed seed. In verses 9-17, Paul invites us to look at the difference between the counterfeit and the real:

For I think that God has displayed us, the apostles, last, as men condemned to death; for we have been made a spectacle to the world, both to angels and to men. We are fools for Christ's sake, but you are wise in Christ! We are weak, but you are strong! You are distinguished, but we are dishonored! Even to the present hour we both hunger and thirst, and we are poorly clothed, and beaten, and homeless. And we labor, working with our own hands. Being reviled, we bless; being persecuted, we endure it; being defamed, we entreat. We have been made as the filth of the world, the offscouring of all things until now. I do not write these things to shame you, but as my beloved children I warn you. For though you might have ten thousand instructors in Christ, yet you do not have many fathers; for in Christ Jesus I have begotten you through the gospel. Therefore I urge you, imitate me. For this reason I have sent Timothy to you, who is my beloved and faithful son in the Lord, who will remind you of my ways in Christ, as I teach everywhere in every church.

Jesus said we could discern the real from the counterfeit by fruit. You will know them by their fruit: "...for a tree is known by its fruit"

Matthew 12:33 tells us. Christianity is known by its fruit! Buddhism is known by its fruit! Islam is known by its fruit! Judge for yourself.

Paul proclaimed the marks of a successful ministry and followed the railroad tracks Jesus Himself laid! Jesus embraced the cross and walked in humble obedience. The church seems to be enamored by self-proclaimed apostles, and sometimes prophets, who advertise their giftings while the marks of the cross are notably absent from their lives. Should we be looking at the power gifts? Should we focus on dramatic prophetic displays? Should we be swayed by the number of nations to which a person has ministered? Should we be impressed by how many churches are "under" a man's leadership? Would real apostles recruit churches to come "under" their leadership? Is that biblical servanthood or should we be looking at the humility they walk in based on the adversity endured? For the mark of apostleship, Paul appeals to the magnitude of adversity as the chief authenticity of the reality of his calling. God made him a "father in the faith," but the price tag was a monumental application of the cross.

It is not just an issue of God saying, "I am going to take you into the wilderness." It is the issue of Christlikeness being worked in the heart with *humility* through personal crucifixion. The mark of the cross is the mark of personal crucifixion through adversity that transforms the dictates of the flesh into an attitude of servanthood embracing God's purpose. Without this mark, one can whole-heartedly recruit churches, but once marked, such an endeavor is unthinkable! 2 Corinthians 1:3-7 documents this principle working in the Corinthian church. Historically, they were well-endowed in the gifts of the Spirit, but were quite indifferent to receiving the message of sacrificing for others. Many apparently rejected the message of suffering. Therefore, it made them food for the counterfeit ministries who were promoting themselves. History certainly seems to repeat itself. 2 Corinthians 1:3-7 says:

> *Blessed be the God and Father of our Lord Jesus Christ, the*
> *Father of mercies and God of all comfort, who comforts us*
> *in all our tribulation, that we may be able to comfort those*
> *who are in any trouble, with the comfort with which we*

> *ourselves are comforted by God. For as the sufferings of*
> *Christ abound in us, so our consolation also abounds*
> *through Christ. Now if we are afflicted, it is for your*
> *consolation and salvation, which is effective for enduring the*
> *same sufferings which we also suffer. Or if we are comfort-*
> *ed, it is for your consolation and salvation. And our hope for*
> *you is steadfast, because we know that as you are partakers*
> *of the sufferings, so also you will partake of the consolation.*

Adversity became a mark in Paul's life and he trumpeted it everywhere he went because it was a distinguishing mark. Pseudo-apostles did not have it! Paul was shouting: **the devil does not fight the counterfeit like he does the real.** Jesus was our pattern. When you see great adversity, it usually means the individual is carrying real gold. We need to understand that this mark results from the measure of adversity we walk through as we pursue His "purpose and call" on our lives. If we ask ourselves, "Why does such warfare develop?" then we have to say it comes for the same reason it came to the apostles in the early church. Verses 8-11 say:

> *For we do not want you to be ignorant, brethren, of our*
> *trouble which came to us in Asia: that we were burdened*
> *beyond measure, above strength, so that we despaired even of*
> *life. Yes, we had the sentence of death in ourselves, that we*
> *should not trust in ourselves but in God who raises the dead,*
> *who delivered us from so great a death, and does deliver us;*
> *in whom we trust that He will still deliver us, you also*
> *helping together in prayer for us, that thanks may be given*
> *by many persons on our behalf for the gift granted to us*
> *through many.*

How is it we attempt to walk away (some even decide to run) from the sentence of death God gives? Does this sentence only come that we might be approved—vessels fit for the Master's use? Is it in this place we are marked for ministry and separated from the spirit of mammon which continually consumes people? Mammon may be the major preparational mark for 666. Separating from it brings Christlikeness. In Philippians 2:8-9, we find Jesus walked this out before us:

> *And being found in appearance as a man, He humbled*
> *Himself and became obedient to the point of death, even the*
> *death of the cross. Therefore God also has highly exalted*
> *Him and given Him the name which is above every name....*

The mark of the cross is the path Jesus walked. He came into full authority of God because He was willing to walk the purpose and plan of God unto death. This is the pattern God has established. The mark of the cross is primary in end-time preparation. Leaders either have it or they do not and if they do not, watch out for flesh-eating viruses!

Following this process marks us with a different spirit, enabling us to speak from a higher level of authority. Hear what Paul has to say at the end of his ministry about the number of people who were willing to embrace this path and stand, as he stood, in a place of ministry; delivered from self-seeking, self-service, and self-promotion. Philippians is one of the last books written by the apostle before his death. In Philippians 2:19-21 he says:

> *But I trust in the Lord Jesus to send Timothy to you shortly,*
> *that I also may be encouraged when I know your state. For*
> *I have no one like-minded, who will sincerely care for your*
> *state. For all seek their own, not the things which are of*
> *Christ Jesus.*

Timothy embraced the cross to the same level as Paul. How much cross are we willing to embrace? At the end of his life and ministry, Paul had a very few people who had embraced the cross and walked it out to the point where they could stand together. To walk with Paul, you had to depart from self-serving and embrace God-serving. Paul refused to disciple individual kingdom-builders. A handful of people over a lifetime are not very many. What we are talking about here is a pathway for ministry that the majority apparently refuse to walk. Is it any wonder we read in Philippians 3:17-21:

> *Brethren, join in following my example, and note those who*
> *so walk, as you have us for a pattern. For many walk, of*
> *whom I have told you often, and now tell you even weeping,*
> *that they are the enemies of the cross of Christ: whose end is*
> *destruction, whose god is their belly, and whose glory is in*

> *their shame—who set their mind on earthly things. For our citizenship is in heaven, from which we also eagerly wait for the Savior, the Lord Jesus Christ, who will transform our lowly body that it may be conformed to His glorious body, according to the working by which He is able even to subdue all things to Himself.*

Paul did not say that many walked as the enemies of Christ, but he did say they walked as "…enemies of the cross of Christ." Apparently, we can spend a lifetime working for Jesus, speaking for Him, recruiting for Him, and still be enemies of the cross. We can still say "no" to the application of the cross when it comes. This is something Paul had witnessed many times during his life. God had chosen a path for him that very few were willing to follow. The process, of course, brought adversity to the point of despairing even of life. How many times did Paul find himself in a place of impossibility and yet chose to continue walking in God's purpose, knowing full well it was bringing him to the end of himself? This is the issue of the application of the cross. Hebrews 11 is a wonderful place to read about victories birthed through faith by great men and women of God, yet Hebrews, chapter 11 has a whole section about those who refused deliverance from adversity in order that they might find "…a better resurrection." Verses 32-35 state:

> *And what more shall I say? For the time would fail me to tell of Gideon and Barak and Samson and Jephthah, also of David and Samuel and the prophets: who through faith subdued kingdoms, worked righteousness, obtained pro- mises, stopped the mouths of lions, quenched the violence of fire, escaped the edge of the sword, out of weakness were made strong, became valiant in battle, turned to flight the armies of the aliens. Women received their dead raised to life again. And others were tortured, not accepting deliverance, that they might obtain a better resurrection.*

Can we raise up a generation that is willing to walk in this level of the application of the cross, where their adversity is unto death, and yet they refuse deliverance in order to obtain "…a better resurrection"? In our "instant" society, how can we raise this level of commitment to the Lord if we do not embrace it ourselves? Paul had numerous opportunities to throw in the towel. He even lists them over in 2 Corinthians 11:23-29. When fighting for his apostleship, he lists the intensity of the adversity:

> *Are they ministers of Christ? —I speak as a fool—I am more: in labors more abundant, in stripes above measure, in prisons more frequently, in deaths often. From the Jews five times I received forty stripes minus one. Three times I was beaten with rods; once I was stoned; three times I was shipwrecked; a night and a day I have been in the deep; in journeys often, in perils of waters, in perils of robbers, in perils of my own countrymen, in perils of the Gentiles, in perils in the city, in perils in the wilderness, in perils in the sea, in perils among false brethren; in weariness and toil, in sleeplessness often, in hunger and thirst, in fastings often, in cold and nakedness—besides the other things, what comes upon me daily: my deep concern for all the churches. Who is weak, and I am not weak? Who is made to stumble, and I do not burn with indignation?*

Paul walked through an amazing magnitude of adversity, and throughout the process he attributes it to God's purpose and plan in his life, in order that grace received to endure becomes strength made perfect in weakness. His heart is transformed and he becomes a vessel of honor delivered from self-indulgence, self-promotion, personal kingdom-building and the entire spectrum of what mammon offers. How can it be, that when judging the emergence of the apostolic anointing in the church today, we generally look at everything except the adversity an individual has endured? In Paul's understanding, based on what he ministered to the church, if you judge somebody to have an apostolic anointing, you should look at their life and find evidence of an apostolic price. The cross draws blood! It is an unsettling sight when accurately viewed. Like Jesus in Isaiah 53, there is nothing to be desired. Nobody in their right mind volunteers for this, you can only get drafted!

The apostle Peter wrote two epistles. In 1 Peter chapter 4, we recognize that Peter also knew the mark of which Paul speaks. Beginning in verse 12, he says:

Beloved, do not think it strange concerning the fiery trial
which is to try you, as though some strange thing happened
to you; but rejoice to the extent that you partake of Christ's
sufferings, that when His glory is revealed, you may also be
glad with exceeding joy. If you are reproached for the name
of Christ, blessed are you, for the Spirit of glory and of God
rests upon you. On their part He is blasphemed, but on your
part He is glorified.

Did Peter learn this by personal example? Peter understood
adversity was not strange; it was, in fact, the norm, and you could
expect the same level of adversity which paralleled your calling. We
should eventually realize God is preparing us in proportion to the
magnitude of what we have asked of Him. It appears that the degree
to which we ask to impact the kingdom of darkness is the same
degree to which Satan has legal right to test and try us. How can we
continue complaining when we asked for it? Paul understood this
and walked it out. Jesus understood the principle. Peter understood
it. Jesus even told the Twelve they did not know what they were
asking for because they were not in tune with the parallel baptism of
adversity corresponding to the level for what they were asking.

In Mark 10:35-45, James and John wanted to sit one on the right
and one on the left-hand in His glory. Jesus responded by telling
them they really did not understand the parallel price tag or the level
of crucifixion demanded to grant the request. Peter speaks to the
very same issues. We know this is a universal principle. The early
apostles all understood the process and the generational birthing
cycle to which they were called. The early church fully embraced the
process, while the twenty-first century church seems to be running
from it. You cannot attain the necessary marks for the days ahead
and avoid this process!

Where is your commitment?

Just how far does it reach?

Have you faith to walk out

The devotion you preach?

Will you choose the God-path

Fully walking His way,

When the cost is so great

There are no words to say?

CHAPTER 6

Fullness - God's Ultimate Mark

Presenting Our Forehead

During David's reign, the sons of Issachar according to 1 Chronicles 12:32 had "…understanding of the times, to know what Israel ought to do…." When we realize Satan's number 666 is a counterfeit seal for the demonically dominated, it frees us from the fear of persecution to pursue all nine marks that comprise the true seal. The final application of God's ultimate seal is mentioned in Revelation 22:1-4:

> And he showed me a pure river of water of life, clear as crystal, proceeding from the throne of God and of the Lamb. In the middle of its street, and on either side of the river, was the tree of life, which bore twelve fruits, each tree yielding its fruit every month. And the leaves of the tree were for the healing of the nations. And there shall be no more curse, but the throne of God and of the Lamb shall be in it, and His servants shall serve Him. They shall see His face, and His name shall be on their foreheads.

When Jesus proclaimed the great commission, He emphasized making disciples, not just converts. Receiving the Lord's ultimate seal, His name affixed on our foreheads, is the result of pursuing personal **fullness** in discipleship where we grow into the full measure of commitment and dedication paralleling Jesus' own walk. All who are willing to sow their very lives into accomplishing God's purposes qualify to wear His name. Doing anything that makes God ashamed (Hebrews 11:8-19) disqualifies us from carrying His **fullness**. The process by which we attain the divine seal, His name on our forehead, necessitates a complete understanding of all principles comprising **fullness**. Money is a commodity we carry for one purpose—exchange of goods and services (Economics 101). In the realm of the spirit, when a person yields fully to their God of choice, they become coins, ready to be spent at their Master's direction.

The demons of radical Islam demonstrate daily the commitment of their followers through a continual parade of militaristic suicide bombing attacks. Only the spiritually disturbed are blind enough to attempt negotiating with the demonized. God refused to negotiate with the Amalekites. Government exists as a minister of God executing wrath on evildoers. He ordered them destroyed. Saul lost his kingship (government) for refusing to annihilate them. Perhaps the reason God is restoring David's heart to the church is that the world is facing demonized Amalekites. Will the church ever yield to the Lord a level of dedication that parallels what the enemy receives from his recruits? Why are the demonized doing a better job of discipling than the church? We must choose the spiritual status of change in God's pocket. The pinnacle passion of discipleship is a life spent purchasing an eternal purpose. 2 Peter 3:10-12 outlines our Father's ultimate goal. When we volunteer to be spent **purchasing** a new heavens and earth, and understanding the price of such a purchase, we not only achieve parity with the first generation church, but qualify to wear our Master's name on our foreheads.

The price of generational parity (matching the early church) emerges clearly when we study the foundational principles (seen in Genesis to Revelation) of **fullness**. These passages will probably be unmarked in your Bibles even if we are the most diligent of daily readers because they have been hidden for a "yet to be marked" generation! God reveals His plans and purposes to Davidic forerunner generations, that they may prepare their successors to build and complete the vision. If we want a generation prepared to wear the name of Jesus, we must lead them to embrace God's principles of **fullness**.

The concept of **fullness** usually dictates the major prophetic transitions in scripture. If we combine understanding **fullness** with a comprehension of what the early church taught, we would be tilling the spiritual soil and planting for a "sons of Issachar" harvest. Only a clear understanding of times and seasons will keep us from tangents in this hour.

The concept of **fullness** emerges as we investigate a family of Greek words, which in their entirety paint a portrait of God's ways, purposes and the path toward being marked. **Play-ro-mah**,[8] the third derivative from the root, is a noun meaning, "that of which a thing is full, to complete or fill to the top until no space remains." The second derivative from the root is **play-ro-o**. It is a verb and it means, "to fill or fulfill." **Play-race** is the first derivative. It is an adjective and it means the sense of being filled. The root is **play-tho** and is defined as, "what fully takes possession of the mind is said to fill it."

Galatians 4:4 presents an excellent picture of **play-ro-mah** as it relates to prophetic transition and fulfillment. Galatians 4:4-5 says:

> *But when the fullness of the time had come, God sent forth His Son, born of a woman, born under the law, to redeem those who were under the law, that we might receive the adoption as sons.*

In Galatians 4:4, the Greek word for time is **chronos** and it generally means that which has a set beginning or a set ending and can be numbered by the calendar or clock. Galatians 4:4 reveals God's sovereign hand as seen in shaping history to bring forth His Son at the perfect time. God used both believers and unbelievers in this preparational process.

The prophet Daniel saw this heavenly hand and spoke accordingly in chapter 2:31-35:

> *You, O king, were watching; and behold, a great image! This great image, whose splendor was excellent, stood before you; and its form was awesome. This image's head was of fine gold, its chest and arms of silver, its belly and thighs of bronze, its legs of iron, its feet partly of iron and partly of clay. You watched while a stone was cut out without hands,*

which struck the image on its feet of iron and clay, and broke them in pieces. Then the iron, the clay, the bronze, the silver, and the gold were crushed together, and became like chaff from the summer threshing floors; the wind carried them away so that no trace of them was found. And the stone that struck the image became a great mountain and filled the whole earth.

Daniel literally saw the sovereignty of God manifested in a vision. He saw the majesty of the neo-Babylonian empire as headed by Nebuchadnezzar. He saw the ascension of the neo-Persian empire represented by the silver chest and arms, which Cyrus established in 539 BC of which Isaiah 45 speaks. The third power to ascend the throne was represented by the bronze belly and thighs and was established by Alexander the Great in 330 BC.

Alexander the Great was unique in that he understood great warriors always spend their lives building an empire for the next generation. Alexander is a good example of God using unbelievers. He knew he would not live to see the fruit of all conquests made. Someone else would probably enjoy the work of his hands. So in an attempt to leave a legacy, he began to establish a policy whereby he encouraged his troops to intermarry with the conquered women from each region, thus establishing a garrison in each location, and decreeing that only Greek would be spoken as the language of commerce. If you wanted to do business, you had to do business in Greek. Only Greek would be spoken in the homes of the troops. Alexander set policies in motion which would make Greek the universal language by the time of Christ. Alexander made one fatal mistake, however. In his zeal to lead by example and encourage his troops to intermarry, he sampled one too many conquests, contracted syphilis, and died at age 33—oops! Without Alexander, the spread of the gospel would have been greatly hindered.

The fourth thing Daniel saw was the Roman Empire, which had iron legs and feet of clay mixed with iron. Some believe this to be the latter day confederation from which the Antichrist rules. The regression in value and strength of metal in the vision from gold to silver to bronze to iron to clay indicates a steadily decreasing power in grandeur. Nebuchadnezzar was an absolute despot whose whim determined life or death. Not so four hundred plus years later when Rome came to Palestine with its Senate, Assemblies and democratic checks and balances so common to the Greeks. Rome was much more interested in military preservation. Their paramount goal was building roads so the military could traverse the empire, keeping insurrection down. We see the hand of an omnipotent God moving upon men to accomplish a preparation in history. God brought His Son on the scene at the perfect moment, when for the first time there was a universal language and ready travel from one point of the empire to another. The real meaning of **play-ro-mah** as it impacts history is readily seen in the preparation of history to receive the Son of God.

As President of the United States, General Dwight Eisenhower proposed an interstate highway system for America based on his knowledge and understanding of Roman military history. As it is today, during a time of national crisis, the interstate system can be declared inaccessible to the average citizen, being reserved strictly for military transport.

A look at history releases a definite awe concerning God's ability to structure situation and circumstance, as a farmer would prepare a field for planting, for the perfect time to sow the seed and reap the greatest harvest. This is the setting for understanding Galatians 4:4:

> *But when the fullness of the time* [chro-nos] *had come, God sent forth His Son, born of a woman, born under the law, to redeem those who were under the law, that we might receive the adoption as sons.*

The word **chro-nos** indicates a set time, measurable by clock or calendar, a date in history that God chose based on His foreknowledge of human response to divine interaction.

In John 7:1-8, we see another Greek word for time, **kai-ros**:

> *After these things Jesus walked in Galilee; for He did not want to walk in Judea, because the Jews sought to kill Him. Now the Jews' Feast of Tabernacles was at hand. His brothers therefore said to Him, "Depart from here and go into Judea, that Your disciples also may see the works that You are doing. For no one does anything in secret while he*

*himself seeks to be known openly. If you do these things, show Yourself to the world. For even His brothers did not believe in Him. Then Jesus said to them, "My time has not yet come, but your time is always ready. The world cannot hate you, but it hates Me because I testify of it that its works are evil. You go up to this feast. I am not yet going up to this feast, for My **time** [kai-ros] has not yet fully come."*

Kai-ros presents an entirely different concept of time. It is time not measured by a set beginning or a set ending, as **chro-nos**, but **kai-ros** is instead marked by the thumbprint of what God does over a season until that print is readily recognizable. We consistently use this concept, often without realization. We name past periods by what God made prominent, i.e., Azusa Street, the Healing Revival, the Charismatic Renewal or the Laughing Revival. In naming a season by what God did during that period, we are actually using the **kai-ros** concept. A **kai-ros** is much more definable by the character of the divine intervention than when it began or ended.

Numerous times in the New Testament, a leadership season of 40 years is called a **chronos**. It is measurable. It has a set beginning and set ending. The interesting thing about John 7:1-8 is that Jesus does not use **chro-nos** but **kai-ros**. Jesus said, "...My **kai-ros** has not yet **fully** come." **Kai-ros**, therefore, can define the variable space of time necessary to accomplish a preassigned task.

Contrasting Galatians 4:4 with John 7:8 helps us understand the two different concepts of time reflected by the different words, **kai-ros** and **chro-nos**, and becomes a foundation then to understand Acts 3:19-21. This passage presents a framework to view the activity of the Holy Spirit interacting with the church during the last century. Acts 3:19-21 says:

*Repent therefore and be converted, that your sins may be blotted out, so that times [kai-roi] of refreshing may come from the presence of the Lord, and that He may send Jesus Christ, who was **preached to you** before, whom heaven must receive until the times [chro-non] of restoration of **all** things, which God has spoken by the mouth of **all** His holy prophets since the world began.*

The intriguing part of this passage is that both **kai-roi** and **chro-non** are plural. Verse 19 then tells us when there are moves in repentance, we open the door for times/**kai-roi** of refreshing to come from the presence of the Lord. Verse 21 declares God gives to the church times, plural, more than one/**chro-non** of restoration.

Acts 7:30 says, "When forty years was full to him...." Acts 13:18 shows the same concept saying, "Now for a **chro-nos** of about 40 years..." proving **chro-nos** carries the concept of a 40-year leadership generation. During the twentieth century, we completed two unique 40-year **chro-nos** leadership generations, each one having distinct and multiple **kai-ros** moves of God. When the Holy Spirit was poured out in the early 1900's, God raised up a leadership generation from about 1906 to 1908 that lasted for 40 years. A number of those leaders began to depart during the transition period, with 1948 being a sort of center-pole year, plus or minus ten years. From 1938 to 1958, there was a dramatic leadership change. A healing revival began in 1948. A prophetic move started shortly thereafter called "Latter Rain." A tremendous evangelistic move began for the evangelical church as Billy Graham and others experienced a dramatic anointing of the Holy Spirit for evangelism. The last forty also included the Charismatic, Faith and Worship (Tabernacle of David) movements.

History records a minimum of seven distinctive **kai-ros** thumbprint moves of God during the second leadership **chro-nos** of the twentieth century. It may be that we can expect about seven distinct **kai-ros** outpourings over the next 40-year leadership generation. Just as **fullness** governs a **chro-nos** leadership generation, so does it govern a **kai-ros** thumbprint outpouring. John 7 indicates that Jesus could not go to the feast because **fullness** had not yet been accomplished in His ministry, even though it was merely a few days away. Do you feel prepared to finish your race in the face of persecution unto death?

Three "Second" Comings

The chief issue of Acts 3 becomes a framework for the wrapping up of the age and the fulfillment of prophetic promise. The significance of Acts 3:19-21 can be seen when we place its prophetic proclamation as initiating the three progressive comings of the Lord revealed in the New Testament after the ascension. The church talks only about the **Second Coming**, but there are three "second" comings in the New Testament. The comings of the Lord in order from last to first are: third **"with us,"** second **"for us"** and first **"to us."**

The third and final coming is Jude, verse 14:

> *Now Enoch, the seventh from Adam, prophesied about these men also, saying, "Behold, the Lord comes with ten thousands of His saints...."*

The last of the three comings of Jesus is **with** the church for the purpose of judgment.

The middle **second coming**, and perhaps most familiar, is in 1 Thessalonians 4:17, **"for us."**

> *Then we who are alive and remain shall be caught up together with them in the clouds to meet the Lord in the air. And thus we shall always be with the Lord.*

This coming is for His saints, and is often referred to as "the rapture." If we emphasize the rapture two or three decades prior to its **kai-ros**, we hurt the church and help the devil hide the current coming for which we should be preparing. By trumpeting rapture out of season, the enemy effectively masks the marking of believers. We do not prepare for what we are not expecting. Several decades ago, the Lord said to me, "You expect the Jesus Peter, James and John got, and Peter, James and John expected the Jesus you are going to get." I had always enjoyed anticipating the rapture. This was my first clue God might demand prior preparation to accomplish prophetic purpose. God knows how to "jerk the slack" out of our eschatology!

In order, the three comings of Jesus after the ascension are **"to you," "for you"** and **"with you."** The first coming before the rapture is in Acts 3:19 where Jesus comes "to the church" to empower us for paying the price to wind up the age and gather what appears to be an end-time harvest. How is it we have so many segments of the church looking **"for us"** when "all" prophecies spoken by "all" prophets have not yet been fulfilled (verse 21)? We could easily miss what God is doing by expecting the wrong visitation. If we avoid duplicating the assumptions of the scribes and Pharisees, perhaps we will be prepared. In Jesus' generation, their prophetic assumptions blinded them to God's visitation. God came to visit and they did not recognize Him. They were looking for Jesus the Judge. We are looking for Jesus the Savior. How much is God doing now, that we do not see? Are we about to repeat the worst mistakes of the first century because we are looking for the wrong visitation? It would appear so! Do we know Jesus the Judge? Can we move His hand against today's Amalekites? If not, we are way below the level at which we should be functioning! (see *The Sure Mercies of David*).

Looking for the Wrong Rapture?

Matthew 12:29 says:

> *Or else how can one enter a strong man's house and plunder his goods, unless he first binds the strong man? And then he will plunder his house.*

The New Testament speaks of two different "catching aways." One is done by Jesus. The other is done by the church. What the church does to the devil will be more dramatic than what Jesus does for the church. The Greek word used here for spoil or plunder is **har-paz-ai** meaning to "snatch up or away, to seize or carry off by force, to rapture. The word often denotes the emotion of a sudden swoop, and usually that of a force which cannot be resisted."[9] It means to make a clean sweep of all that is in the house.[10] Jesus used a much stronger word in verse 29 **(novum testamentum graece)** when He said, "And then **he will plunder** his house." When strengthening a concept in Greek, prefixes are often added to the root word which is the case here. Jesus added **dia** for dramatic emphasis. **Dia-har-paz-ai** is the Greek word demonstrating dramatic increase of force or divine display.

Two different Greek words convey a picture of appropriation by force: **klep-to** meaning to sneak away with goods stolen in the darkness or privately where no eye sees versus **har-paz-o** which is to execute an appropriation publicly where every eye can see as a demonstration of superior authority and power. The rapture passage of 1 Thessalonians 4:17 uses only the weaker basic form from **har-**

paz-o. When Jesus chooses **dia-har-paz-o**, He thunders a clear message: What the church does to the devil in fulfilling Psalm 2:8, "Ask of Me and I will give you the nations..." is much more of a dramatic display than Jesus catching away the church. It seems our would-be prophecy teachers have emphasized the wrong rapture. Who in their right mind would want to be snatched away in what is clearly a secondary event prior to the church snatching away from the enemy, resources, cities and nations—which appears to be the primary event?

In Christ Jesus, the deceived and banished race of Genesis 3 must execute the written judgment and prove to all heavenly hosts the wisdom of God in a victorious demonstration. God intends to make a point. The harvest must reach **fullness!** You and I, as members of the church, are the ones to execute it! The problem is, only marked believers qualify. Let's pursue God's mark and qualify. How can we represent Jesus the Judge if we do not know Him? How can we participate with Jesus who makes war? The answer is in the Davidic Psalms and praying them. (*Sure Mercy* reveals how to pray.)

Isaiah must be shaking his head in prophetic disbelief at the biblical discernment displayed by some segments of today's church. The mere prospect of a people so willing to forego such great promises as, "...ask of Me and I will give you the nations..." by embracing an "escape at any cost" mentality (rapture) must make the prophets weep for our generation. Can't you hear their voices? Samuel must be crying in disbelief at today's weasels masquerading as leaders. He hacked Agag into pieces because Saul refused to at God's direction! I imagine Samuel shaking his head in disbelief at today's wimpy, refusing to execute justice—church!

The "bless-me club" mentality is having a dramatic effect on many segments of the church. If we judge the doctrine by the fruit it is producing currently, we would have to say it is truly damaging many segments of Christ's body. When "pandering to people" results in diminished discipling of the next generation and never confronts the dictates of their flesh, we have retreated from God's harvest field. Discerning the origin of a doctrine by the fruit it produces, in this case, should generate a fairly strong adverse reaction. Is seeker-sensitive Christianity preparing a generation to walk with Jesus the Judge and war against enemies of the harvest? Someone fed the American church a tranquilizer and they appear fast asleep. How many terrorists' attacks do we need to have on American soil before we wake up to war—Jesus style? Not Jesus in the gospels—Jesus in Revelation!

We need to understand the concept of the "last days" as presented in the New Testament. When Peter stood up to preach on the day of Pentecost to explain what God was doing among the 120, he used the terminology "the last days" to explain God's purpose. Peter said in Acts 2:17-21:

> *And it shall come to pass **in the last days**, says God, That I will pour out of My Spirit on all flesh; Your sons and your daughters shall prophesy, Your young men shall see visions, Your old men shall dream dreams. And on My menservants and on My maidservants I will pour out My Spirit in those days; And they shall prophesy. I will show wonders in heaven above And signs in the earth beneath: Blood and fire and vapor of smoke. The sun shall be turned into darkness, And the moon into blood, Before the coming of the great and notable day of the Lord. And it shall come to pass that whoever calls on the name of the Lord shall be saved.*

Two thousand years ago Peter said, "We are in the last days." Revelation 19:11 reveals Jesus in the last days, "...He judges and makes war." Have you prepared to walk with Jesus the Judge? Are you "marked" and ready to war with the King of kings? The time to grow up is now. If you feel totally unprepared in this realm, you can parallel my developmental path by listening to the CD series entitled "God and War," followed by "Sure Mercies," then "The Path, Price & Power of the Plumbline" then "Spiritual Judicial Authority," then "Jesus & Justice," and then "A Heart for War."

How Old Will You Be When…?

In some pockets of the church, "rapture now" thinking is so pervasive that perhaps we should attempt to gauge in scripture how close or far we are in our generation from this prophetic event to confirm the necessity of gaining all God's marks! This exercise can only be called the "big guess" and is presented just for fun. Luke 21:20-24 is the place to start for such a "guestimate."

> *But when you see Jerusalem surrounded by armies, then know that its desolation is near. Then let those in Judea flee to the mountains, let those who are in the midst of her depart, and let not those who are in the country enter her. For these are the days of vengeance, that all things which are written may be fulfilled. But woe to those who are pregnant and to those who are nursing babies in those days! For there will be great distress in the land and wrath upon this people. And they will fall by the edge of the sword, and be led away captive into all nations. And Jerusalem will be trampled by Gentiles until the times of the Gentiles are fulfilled.*

Jerusalem was surrounded by armies nearly forty years after Jesus was rejected. The warning He gave was fulfilled in 70 AD. We are not excluding a secondary prophetic fulfillment of this passage in any way, shape or form, but merely pointing out that Jesus was dealing with three questions in Matthew 23, 24 and 25.

The three questions concerned judgment on the temple and its being torn down. Jesus said, "…not one stone would remain upon another…" in the temple. The three questions were, "Tell us, when will these things be? And what will be the sign of Your coming, and of the end of the age?" The three questions were obvious, and they referred first and foremost to the destruction of Jerusalem which He prophesied. Secondly, what would be the sign of His coming, and third, what would be the sign of the end of the age? Matthew 24 and 25 contain Jesus' answers to these questions. One question pertained to the destruction of Jerusalem and we need to realize Luke 21:23 had a very dramatic and definite application. A potential timeline based on specific assumption may emerge from Luke 21:24b and 29-33:

> *…And Jerusalem will be trampled by Gentiles until the times of the Gentiles are fulfilled… . And He spoke to them a parable: 'Look at the fig tree, and all the trees. When they are already budding, you see and know for yourselves that summer is now near. So you, likewise, when you see these things happening, know that the kingdom of God is near.*

Assuredly, I say to you, this generation will by no means pass away till all things are fulfilled. Heaven and earth will pass away, but My words will by no means pass away.

If verse 32 specifically speaks to, and qualifies verse 24, "Jerusalem being trampled underfoot until the Gentiles are fulfilled," then we can do some simple math and set a potential date for the winding up of the age and the fulfillment of prophecy. If verse 32, like an adjective qualifies verse 24, then the beginning date would be established when the Jews fully regained control of Jerusalem. While Israel became a nation in 1948, for a number of years Jerusalem was still partitioned and divided, and the Jewish nation did not have the entire city under their control for nearly 20 years. It was not until the Six Day War of 1967 that all of Jerusalem became one again under the control of the Jewish nation. If verse 32 qualifies verse 24, and if the city of Jerusalem will never be overwhelmed and taken again, then we can make some very interesting projections about the winding up of the age.

Our baseline year would have to begin in 1967. Jesus said this generation would not pass away. We would have to assume that the generation was born in that year. It took 30 years for people to mature to the place God would set them in office for leadership. Their leadership generation then lasted, generally speaking, 40 years. In Genesis 15, a generation is also spoken of as occupying a hundred-year span. We have some big "if's" by which we POSTULATE a date to look at for the winding up of the age. The year 1967 plus 70 puts us at 2037 if we are allowed to use 70 years for a generation. If there is a seven-year tribulation period as a grand finale, then in order to project how long our potential future in ministry might be, assuming a pre-trib rapture, we need to ask ourselves how old will we be in the year 2030. Will we have enough time to have a family and raise kids? Will our offspring have enough time to contribute to the Kingdom of God?

If the rapture does not take place until 2030 (2060, using a 100-year generation), how old will we be then and what difference will the rapture make, if any, in our lives? These are strong serious questions we need to ask ourselves concerning our future and the purpose of God for His Kingdom. If we are expecting the rapture in the next few years and it does not come until 2030 or 2060, how much will we forfeit by being out of sync with God's timing? Aren't we supposed to know the times and seasons? Where is the anointing for the sons of Issachar? During the transition from Saul to David, the sons of Issachar "...had understanding of the times, to know what Israel ought to do...." We are always safe when we concentrate on growth and choose to pour ourselves into discipleship!

While some would argue God could wind up the age sooner than later, there is a very simple projection that leads most contemplative individuals to believe it will be later rather than sooner. Government population statistics reveal it has taken 6000 years for world population to reach the one billion mark in 1900. It took another fifty years to reach two billion. By the year 2,000, we were looking at four, and by 2020, eight. We face the prospect of having a harvest of people living in the earth greater than the sum of all our predecessors combined. We are looking at a future when more people will live on the earth at one time than have ever died on the earth in its cumulative history. Knowing the "Father-heart" of God, does not that speak volumes about the future of a great harvest?

There is a harvest to reap and a generation to prepare for such a season. In addition, we have all the unfulfilled prophecies given by all the prophets which are too numerous to include. In Acts 3:19-21, Jesus personally guarantees fulfillment of all prophecies given by all the prophets.

LORD, Please Put Us on the Same Page

When we look at what God has done in just the past century with the church, it appears obvious He has very consistently been pursuing the equipping of a generation to bring in a mighty harvest. Focusing on the rapture hinders rather than helps. We could accomplish the discipling of nations if our churches could get in one accord.

There is a very consistent thread that runs through all three **chronos** leadership generations of the twentieth century. This thread comes from Acts 2:33-35:

> *Therefore being exalted to the right hand of God, and having received from the Father the promise of the Holy Spirit, He poured out this which you now see and hear. For David did*

not ascend into the heavens, but he says himself: "The Lord said to my Lord, 'Sit at My right hand, till I make Your enemies Your footstool.'"

Azusa Street marked a restoration of the outpouring of the Holy Spirit. The specific purpose was to empower the church to extend the kingdom of God and realize an appointed dimension of making our enemies our footstool. If we take a panoramic look at the twentieth century, we have to say within each distinctive leadership **chro-nos** (40-year period) that God has specifically begun to empower ever greater numbers of His church. When the Azusa Street Move encompassed the earth and became denominationalized, those remaining untouched were visited during the second **chro-nos** (40 years) leadership generation in a wholly different and distinct way called the Charismatic Renewal, but the result was the same. The Charismatic Renewal could be characterized by a season when God's boot camp of the Holy Spirit found many who were not even seeking the experience. God broadened the circle. Why would God spend a century empowering ever greater numbers of His church? Perhaps the single greatest reason for receiving the Holy Spirit is accepting a distinguishing seal, significantly marking each person.

The third leadership generation began about 1988 and will probably not be finished until about 2028, if we last that long. Again, the church has experienced a major **kai-ros** move of God, whose chief focus has been to impact thousands of untouched evangelicals, as the power of the Holy Spirit marches on. This has certainly been the testimony of the "Toronto Blessing" throughout Europe.

We can postulate one of God's chief purposes in every **chro-nos** leadership generation is to empower His people to accomplish divine purposes. The New Testament speaks clearly about the issue of **fullness**. In Acts 7:23, the Greek text literally says: "When the **chro-nos** of 40 years was filled to him...." Verse 30 in Greek says, "And being fulfilled years 40." Acts 13:18, describing Moses' third 40-year period, says: "Now for a **chro-nos** of about 40 years," demonstrating God's view of a leadership generation. The concept of **fullness** seems to be the governing factor in the coming of Jesus, and as we grow to understand the difference between **kai-ros** and **chro-nos**, we will not be conned into believing specific return dates that people project out of their own mind as being "inspired" by the Lord. Revelation 3:1-2 shows us something very interesting about the concept of **fullness**. Just as God brings a preparational season to **fullness**, which in Moses' life was 40 years, so **fullness** governs our individual lives in God's purpose and plan. Revelation 3:1-2 says:

> *And to the angel of the church in Sardis write, "These things says He who has the seven Spirits of God and the seven stars: 'I know your works, that you have a name that you are alive, but you are dead. Be watchful, and strengthen the things which remain, that are ready to die, for I have not found your works perfect [play-roo] before God.'"*

The Greek word translated perfect is **play-ro-o** meaning "to accomplish, fill up or complete." It shows **fullness** not only governs **chro-nos** leadership generations, but also dictates **kai-ros** thumbprint moves of God and determines our personal contribution to God's purpose and plan in the earth. God has taken a century just attempting to get the church on the same page.

The Price of Fullness

In Acts 24, we discover that reaching **fullness** can carry a tremendous personal price. Willingness to pay this price separates, within a generation, those who qualify for wearing God's name from those who do not. The willingness to pay the price is the qualifying mark in any given generation.

Acts 24:22-27 states:

> *But when Felix heard these things, having more accurate knowledge of the Way, he adjourned the proceedings and said, "When Lysias the commander comes down, I will make a decision on your case." So he commanded the centurion to keep Paul and to let him have liberty, and told him not to forbid any of his friends to provide for or visit him.*
>
> *And after some days, when Felix came with his wife Drusilla, who was Jewish, he sent for Paul and heard him concerning the faith in Christ. Now as he reasoned about righteousness, self-control, and the judgment to come, Felix was afraid and answered, "Go away for now; when I have a*

convenient time [kai-ros] *I will call for you." Meanwhile he also hoped that money would be given him by Paul, that he might release him. Therefore he sent for him more often and conversed with him. But after two years Porcius Festus succeeded Felix; and Felix, wanting to do the Jews a favor, left Paul bound.*

Acts 24:27 says: "But after two full years were completed [**play-ro-tha-sis**] to him." The apostle Paul knew he was headed for Rome and that he had to give a testimony to kings and others in authority. In verse 25 we find Paul ministering to Felix, and Felix, looking for a "...convenient **kairos**," sent him back to confinement hoping money would be given and then he would turn Paul loose.

Paul paid two full years out of his own life for **fullness** to come in judgment to Felix for his greed. **Fullness** can carry a tremendous price tag that is paid in personal captivity for days, weeks, months or years. This became Paul's testimony. Paul spent two years locked up waiting for the cup to fill. **Fullness** in situations like Paul's is a two-edged sword. Believers suffered throughout the season of grace extended to the world. Are we willing to pay the price of **fullness** as God's grace extends to nations?

Nowhere in the New Testament is the Second Coming of Jesus ever spoken of as a **chro-nos**. It is only spoken of as being a **kai-ros**. This speaks volumes, because a **chro-nos** has a set beginning and a set ending, describing a date on the calendar, whereas a **kai-ros** is always God's thumbprint, no set beginning and no set ending, but mostly known by what God does during that season. A **kai-ros** is the character and nature of a God imprint upon the church to accomplish eternal purposes. 2 Peter 3:8-13 brings clarity over judging prophecy concerning the return of Jesus when dates are involved.

2 Peter 3:8-13 says:

But, beloved, do not forget this one thing, that with the Lord one day is as a thousand years, and a thousand years as one day. The Lord is not slack concerning His promise, as some count slackness, but is long-suffering toward us, not willing that any should perish but that all should come to repentance. But the day of the Lord will come as a thief in *the night, in which the heavens will pass away with a great noise, and the elements will melt with fervent heat; both the earth and the works that are in it will be burned up. Therefore, since all these things will be dissolved, what manner of persons ought you to be in holy conduct and godliness, looking for and **hastening** the coming of the day of God, because of which the heavens will be dissolved being on fire, and the elements will melt with fervent heat? Nevertheless we, according to His promise, look for new heavens and a new earth in which righteousness dwells.*

Verse 12 says we can *hasten* the coming of the day of God. If we can hasten it by raising up a generation committed to birthing **fullness**, we can also prolong it (by preaching rapture, rapture, rapture). If we can hasten or prolong it, it therefore must be fluid. Since nowhere in the New Testament is the Second Coming of the Lord spoken of as a **chro-nos**, but only a **kai-ros**, *anyone who projects a date is simply speculating.* The Second Coming of the Lord is fluid. According to Acts 3:19-21, it is dependent on the church recognizing, embracing and fulfilling the appointed prophetic **kai-ros** moves of God. It has no set date and is therefore dependent on the church walking in obedience and fulfilling the prophetic promises of scripture. When anyone comes and says, "Watch out for the year 2012, 2020, or 2030," all you have to do is remember that all the dates projected during the last century were wrong! When standing in the presence of one who is setting a date, you can confidently proclaim, "You, my friend, probably do not know your **kai-ros** from your **chro-nos**." The *Second Coming* is dependent on fulfilling prophetic promises. Psalm 2:8 guarantees nations for the asking. The problem with asking for nations is the Elymas type resistance that can be overcome by a kingly anointing. To fulfill Psalm 2, we must possess the fullness of what Jesus bought in the atonement. Only by accessing divine justice (see "Jesus & Justice" CD series) can we possess nations. The *Second Coming* is fluid, dependent on one generation embracing a Davidic heart for war and moving God's hand of justice! The *Second Coming* is fluid, dependent on the church birthing the justice of God and representing a Messiah making the Jew jealous. Will we pursue?

There's a new generation

Called to walk safely through,

Who need Spirit-led wisdom

For what I've called them to.

Those seasoned with wisdom

Must sit by their side,

They've experienced the fire

In the furnace been tried.

CHAPTER 7

Individual and Corporate Fullness

Recognizing the mark God wants to apply necessitates embracing the concept of **fullness** as it governs major prophetic transitions in scripture. The early church demonstrated their commitment with lives martyred as seed sown into the foundation of the church, following the example of Jesus and the apostles. Is it possible to birth equal fervor without preparing a generation with the same dedication? The same passion which powered first generation Christians must be an essential driving force in the last generation church. If martyrdom was the seed required to found Christianity, what will be the seed necessary to birth a "new heavens and a new earth where righteousness dwells?" The answer to that question determines how we should train the next generation of believers. What price should we prepare them to pay? If we over-prepare them will they thank us, yet if we under-prepare them will they curse us? Will our children rise up and call us blessed if they face persecution without our preparation? What will they call us if they have to face the opposite for which we prepared them? The choices we make now will determine their response then. There is a biblical pattern answering these questions and dictating a direction.

Genesis 15:7-16 says:

> *Then He said to him, "I am the LORD, who brought you out of Ur of the Chaldeans, to give you this land to inherit it." And he said, "LORD God, how shall I know that I will inherit it?" So He said to him, "Bring Me a three-year-old*

heifer, a three-year-old female goat, a three-year-old ram, a turtledove, and a young pigeon" Then he brought all these to Him and cut them in two, down the middle, and placed each piece opposite the other; but he did not cut the birds in two. And when the vultures came down on the carcasses, Abram drove them away. Now when the sun was going down, a deep sleep fell upon Abram; and behold, horror and great darkness fell upon him. Then He said to Abram: "Know certainly that your descendants will be strangers in a land that is not theirs, and will serve them, and they will afflict them four hundred years. And also the nation whom they serve I will judge; afterward they shall come out with great possessions. Now as for you, you shall go to your fathers in peace; you shall be buried at a good old age. But in the fourth generation they shall return here (NKJV), for the iniquity of the Amorites is not yet full" (KJV).

Coming out of Egypt and going into the Promised Land was a major prophetic transition governed by the concept of **fullness**. God's mercy demands **fullness** before He releases the authority to disinherit and destroy nations. Why should Israel have had to wait until the end of the "fourth generation" before they could possess the land God gave by promise? **Fullness** can be a two-edged sword. When understood and embraced, it paves the way for an awesome display of God's presence manifested to fulfill prophetic promise. When **fullness** is misunderstood or rejected, it can have a devastating impact if you are not prepared for its consequences. The rapture is a great message for evangelism, but if embraced prematurely by the church, it sets up a generation of believers for potential failure if persecution and martyrdom arise. Can you imagine living in Egypt in the second or third generation believing you were leaving any day? They left Egypt at the end of 400 years! This brings us to an interesting point of commitment. Are we willing to be believers who carry the prophetic vision throughout a lifetime, only to pass it on to the next generation for fulfillment? Fullness is very much a distinctive part of the Christian life governing much of what we embrace and experience in the earth. We are not our own. We have been bought with a price, and **fullness** proves it.

The other side of the **fullness** coin is, although Israel was promised the land, they could not possess it until the occupying nation had completely defiled it, filling *the cup of iniquity*. Defiling a nation is a very serious issue. How do we defile a land so completely we can no longer possess it as a God-given inheritance? Leviticus chapters 18 and 20 speak to this very issue. One of the four ways people defile their land is to allow the slaughter of innocent children.

Leviticus 18:21 says:

> *And you shall not let any of your descendants pass through the fire of Molech, nor shall you profane the name of your God: I am the LORD.*

Sacrificing innocent children definitely fills the cup. Abortion was legalized in America by the Supreme Court in "Roe v. Wade" and is now estimated to be responsible for over 50 million deaths. Violating God's Word can present terrible personal and national consequences.

Judgments Are Pictures

God's judgments are all custom-made to fit the sin. Each judgment carries a picture within it—the seed of the sin. When Pharaoh drowned the children, attempting to kill Moses, God brought a customized judgment in repaying the sin. He waited 80 years for the exodus, and not only supernaturally killed every first-born male, but promptly drowned the Egyptian army just as Pharaoh had drowned the Israeli children. The judgment was customized covenantally to **portray** the sin.

When the angels came to check out Sodom, they stayed and ate with Lot's family. Israelites were not allowed to eat with unbelievers probably because of sharing salt, a sign of the covenant. When Lot's wife disobeyed their orders, she violated the very covenant of salt she participated in the night before in her own home; and her judgment became a picture of what she rebelliously disregarded. She became a pillar of salt!

Revelation 16:4-7 clarifies this principle, helping us discern the true origin of particular national tragedies:

*Then the third angel poured out his bowl on the rivers and springs of water, and they became blood. And I heard the angel of the waters saying: "You are righteous, O Lord, The One who is and who was and who is to be, Because You have judged these things. For they have shed the blood of saints and prophets, And You have given them blood to drink. For it is their just due." And I heard another from the altar saying, "Even so, Lord God Almighty, true and righteous are Your **judgments**."*

From Genesis to Revelation, God's principles are unchangeable and immutable. There is a future season where so many Christians are martyred; God has no choice but to respond by giving the perpetrators blood to drink. The judgment of blood to drink reflects the sin, that the perpetrators might be enlightened and hopefully some understand and repent.

Like begets like. Every tree produces after its own kind. In the same measure that you use it shall be measured back to you. God's judgments are not always divinely inflicted, but brought into existence in the fullness of time. The spiritual law of sowing and reaping was initiated for our benefit. If we sow according to godly behavior, we reap blessing. But if we support devastation, it is not that God is expressly sending devastation, but we have opened the doors, invited and demanded its multiplied manifestation.

When a nation permits devastation and death by refusing refuge to unborn children they do not want, **they find they can no longer protect the children they do want.** On the seventh day in the seventh year after "Roe v. Wade," by judicial fiat, became the law of the land, our schools emerged as war zones! On January 29, 1979, a distraught 16-year-old took rifle and scope and began shooting children across from her home at the Cleveland Elementary School in San Diego. It was one of our nation's first mass school shootings. She killed the principal and head custodian and wounded nine children. The fruit of "Roe v. Wade" had begun to manifest. In the midst of, and immediately after an outbreak of school violence, everyone asks— "Why?" Consider the following and try to answer "Why not?" On January 22, 1973, "Roe v. Wade" essentially did to the unborn exactly what "Dred Scott" did to the Negro on March 6, 1857. The Scott decision ruled that Blacks were not legal persons according to the U. S. Constitution. A slave could be bought, sold, used or killed at the owner's discretion, just like the unborn today. "Roe v. Wade" is the "Dred Scott" of our day! What Christian in their right mind would support a "Dred Scott" decision today? How is it that a very high percentage of "Dred Scott" descendents continually vote for a political party which supports today's "Dred Scott?" God's Word cries "repent" and stop the duplicity. Why would a Christian support destroying the land?

Many believers are doing exactly that every time they vote, and just do not discern the difference. As church leaders, we must do everything possible to save God's people from a shocking experience on Judgment Day. We do not want the blood of our own congregations on our hands because we were afraid to declare the whole counsel of God. We must appropriate the courage to say what God says!

The second way a nation defiles its land is to embrace nature worship elevating animals above man and hastening judgment. At one point (a few years ago), if you so much as stole an eagle's egg from its nest, the penalty was a $5,000 fine and/or a year in jail as set by Congress (it may have increased). It was illegal to ship a pregnant lobster regardless of which trimester. The fine was $6,000 and/or a year in jail. Babies are destroyed at will, while animals are protected, demanding judgment. Hollywood produces a steady stream of nature-worshippers continually raising money, attempting to elevate the rights of animals above those of men. The Bible tells us man was given dominion—animals were not. We ought to have regard for God's creation, but giving animal's rights that exceed the rights of unborn children demands judgment.

The real culprit of the Columbine, Santana High School and Virginia Tech shootings was not access to guns. Future "Santanas", "Columbines", and "Virginia Techs" cannot be prevented by gun legislation. The real origin of school shootings is spiritual, and the responsible parties include every pro-abortion president, senator, court justice and legislator in both political parties, not to mention every person who supports them with a vote. We may not personally wield the scalpel that terrorizes the unborn, but by supporting those who keep infanticide a national policy against the unwanted, we are responsible for releasing the spirit of murder and destruction upon our children. Like Lot's wife, we have rebelliously disregarded our covenant of life, opening the doors to the spirit of death now stalking our schools. For the answer to "why," one only need look in the mirror. How can we stop the shooting of innocent children without closing the doors we have opened? The only way to remove the blood from our hands is to **repent!** As long as we support the murder of children we do not want, we cannot keep safe the children we do want! We are the answer to "why," if we support abortion with our votes!

Oppose the Sin or Lose the Land

A third "filler of the cup" is in Leviticus 18:22:

> *You shall not lie with a male as with a woman. It is an abomination.*

There is a major cultural war within the courts and government over legalizing homosexual and lesbian relationships through marriage. The Bible clearly says statutory protection of homosexuality and lesbianism defiles the land until we can no longer defend it! God loves every person caught in the deception of declaring, "They were born with their same-sex preference." The church must demonstrate and extend divine love when encountering members of the homosexual community. 1 Corinthians 6:9-11 has very good news for every believer and every person caught in homosexuality. It says:

> *Do you not know that the unrighteous will not inherit the kingdom of God? Do not be deceived. Neither fornicators, nor idolaters, nor adulterers, nor homosexuals, nor sodomites, nor thieves, nor covetous, nor drunkards, nor revilers, nor extortioners will inherit the kingdom of God.* ***And such were some of you.*** *But you were washed, but you were sanctified, but you were justified in the name of the Lord Jesus and by the Spirit of our God.*

The early church experienced an anointing so deep, it confronted and delivered many who believed they were born with a "same-sex" orientation. The Bible proves that view to be erroneous. Sexual orientation is a choice and Jesus empowers us to make a change through repentance! Those who steadfastly refuse such a change can rapidly reach a seared conscience where no possibility of salvation exists. God has promised to restore and exceed the anointing in which the church was birthed. Until that level of power has been possessed, every individual caught in a "same-sex" lifestyle has the option to exit into eternal life. Make no mistake—the scripture is clear about this issue. TODAY is the day of salvation—procrastinate at your own eternal peril! We also have a biblical mandate to oppose the radical homosexual agenda as public policy, or face the national negative consequences of losing the ability to defend our land guaranteeing the success of future terrorist attacks.

Leviticus 18:25 says:

> *For the land is defiled; therefore I visit the punishment of its iniquity upon it, and the land vomits out its inhabitants.*

We are told not to do these things in verse 28:

> *...the land will vomit us out also when we defile it, as it vomited out the nations that were before us.*

Leviticus 20 is a little stronger and a bit more specific. Verses 1, 4-5 state:

> *Then the LORD spoke to Moses saying, "And if the people of the land should in any way hide their eyes from the man, when he gives some of his descendants to Molech, and they do not kill him, then I will set My face against that man and against his family; and I will cut him off from his people, and all who prostitute themselves with him to commit harlotry with Molech."*

When we see abortions continue, and fail to exercise our ability to stop them, the Scripture is clear about God's opposition to our lives. It is unthinkable that a Christian would ever support a candidate championing abortion or gay rights. It is an issue of covenant. Every individual who votes for a political candidate who supports abortion is guilty of murder by covenantal identification. God set both spiritual and political leadership into position by a Covenant of Salt. Salt, a natural preservative, became a sign of covenantal relationship. Leviticus 2:13 demanded salt as a sign of covenantal relationship be added to all grain offerings. Israel was prohibited from eating with people from heathen cultures presumably because of salt used at the table. The Covenant of Salt dictates you become one with the person you vote for in what they stand for and do in the office for which you voted. Do you want to stand before Jesus and give an account for murdering innocent children?

Verses 6-8 apply to anyone calling the **dial-a-demon** psychic networks, where unsuspecting people choose to open their hearts to demonic spirits, as they progress toward becoming reservoirs for demon-dispensing dump trucks.

> *And the person who turns after mediums and familiar spirits, to prostitute himself with them, I will set My face against that person and cut him off from his people. Sanctify yourselves therefore, and be holy, for I am the LORD your God. And you shall keep My statutes, and perform them: I am the LORD who sanctifies you.*

Verse 9 speaks of rebellion that so permeates the drug culture and captures all who partake:

> For everyone who curses his father or his mother shall surely be put to death. He has cursed his father or his mother. His blood shall be upon him.

Verses 10-21 deal with sexual sin, adultery, incest, and homosexuality. Verses 22-23 are perhaps the most startling in the declaration they make.

> *You shall therefore keep all My statutes and all My judgments, and perform them, that the land where I am bringing you to dwell may not vomit you out. And you shall not walk in the **statutes** of the nation which I am casting out before you; for they commit all these things, and therefore I abhor them.*

When a nation statutorily protects abortion, homosexuality or lesbianism, God sees the people as choosing a process of defiling the land. The first consequence is losing the ability to defend our land by a dangerous depletion and reduction in the military. A dramatic downturn or downsizing in the military results until the nation faces a war they cannot win. Hostile nations who have previously stood alone begin joining forces in opposition. Decisions debilitating combat readiness abound. Bases have been closed and down-sizing has become accepted.

Placing women in combat billets with the introduction of co-ed deployments is having a definite impact. During a recent tour of the Kitty Hawk Aircraft Carrier, I was told about 20 percent of the ships personnel were women. A routine deployment could possibly return with as many as 150 pregnancies. Imagine morning sickness multiplied by high seas!

The first major policy declaration of the Clinton Administration brought "Don't ask, don't tell" to the military. This was the first of several dangerous policy decisions demoralizing and eroding a once-strong military, culminating in a slow steady exodus of essential personnel. Isaiah 3:12 says it well:

> *As for My people, children are their oppressors, And women rule over them. O My people! Those who lead you cause you to err, And destroy the way of your paths.*

Moral failures and terrible leadership examples have proved the necessity of Christians getting involved in government, and show why past generations legislated morality. It tells us why our fore-fathers enacted laws making homosexuality illegal. They very simply wanted to keep the country God had given us, and they understood the fastest way to forfeit it was to allow the land to be defiled and filled with iniquity. The land that once flowed with milk and honey is beginning to show signs of dramatically increasing judgments. Jeremiah proclaimed to Israel in Jeremiah 23:10:

> *For the land is full of adulterers; For because of a curse the land mourns. The pleasant places of the wilderness are dried up. Their course of life is evil, And their might is not right.*

In 2 Chronicles 36:16-18 we see the fruit of a people who refused to change when the Lord confronted them about their activities:

> *But they mocked the messengers of God, despised His words, and scoffed at His prophets, until the wrath of the LORD arose against His people, till there was no remedy. Therefore He brought against them the king of the Chaldeans, who*

> *killed their young men with the sword in the house of their*
> *sanctuary and had no compassion on young man or virgin,*
> *on the aged or the weak; He gave them all into his hand.*
> *And all the articles from the house of God, great and small,*
> *the treasures of the house of the LORD, and the treasures of*
> *the king and of his leaders, all these he took to Babylon.*

Just as the land vomited Israel out, our land will vomit us out if we do not change.

Covenants of Death

How have we fallen to such a place? Compare the commitment of today's college graduates with those of our fathers who were willing to die for their faith and revelation of God-given freedom as they enlisted for World War II.

The representative government in nations like America was established based on a biblical understanding of covenantal principles. When the Pilgrims first departed for America, they made a covenant called the "Mayflower Compact." Previous generations understood covenant, and when they established government, they left the covenantal power of the vote with the people, expecting every individual to exercise due diligence when voting. Genesis 17:1-14 gives us a glimpse of the covenant as God extended it to Abraham. Covenant implied relationship where each party was accountable to the other for the performance of promises made. 1 Samuel 18:3-4 gives us an additional part of the picture concerning covenant where it says:

> *Then Jonathan and David made a covenant, because he loved*
> *him as his own soul. And Jonathan took off the robe that was*
> *on him and gave it to David, with his armor, even to his*
> *sword and his bow and his belt.*

To be in covenant meant you guaranteed your weapons, yourself, your entire house for any season of need when war arose against your covenant partner. NATO (North Atlantic Treaty Organization) today was founded on the same biblical principle of covenant, where we promise our military to aid any member nation who is attacked by a non-NATO member. Most nations, most foreign policy and most lives show semblances of biblical covenantal principle.

Webster's definition of covenant states, "In theology the covenant of works, is that implied in the commands, prohibitions, and promises of God; the promise of God to man, that man's perfect obedience should entitle him to happiness. This do, and live; that do, and die."[11]

What happens when a nation seems to have forgotten the covenantal applications of their origin? If we vote for a president, senator or representative who champions homosexuality and lesbianism, and attempts in every way possible to eradicate the heritage of Christian principle, then we are guilty of the actions of that leader, just as if we had committed them ourselves. We are tied to our elected representatives by covenant because we cast our votes for them. *Uniting ourselves with a lawmaker supporting homosexual marriage based on the spiritual laws of the Altar* (see *Purifying the Altar*) *can open the door for family members to be attacked by that spirit.* If we vote for a president who does everything possible to extend abortion throughout the land and throughout the nations, then the continued shedding of innocent blood accrues to our account just as if we had encouraged it ourselves. 2 John 10 and 11 state:

> *If anyone comes to you and does not bring this doctrine, do*
> *not receive him into your house nor greet him; for he who*
> *greets him shares in his evil deeds.*

Voting for a man or woman exceeds a simple greeting by miles. How long will we share in "evil deeds" demanding judgment? We apparently have had so much of the love of God preached, we have forgotten Jesus is also the Judge of all the earth. Israel walked through a parallel season where they disregarded their covenant and as a result, found themselves in 70 years of captivity. Nehemiah 9:32-38 describes their acknowledgment of sin and renewal of covenant as a seal or mark of new beginning. Verse 38 says:

> *And because of all this, We make a sure covenant, and write*
> *it; And our leaders and our Levites and our priests seal it.*

Their generation learned the necessity of covenant keeping the hard way by suffering judgment through disobedience. Surely, we can learn from their mistakes. The end-time church must demonstrate the seal of covenant keeping. Every Christian who votes for a senator, representative, governor or president who encourages and promotes abortion will have to stand before God and give an account for the river of blood caused during their Administration. How can people who proclaim Jesus continually covenant with demons? A significant number of people in the church are going to have to answer for the pollution and destruction of nations based on the covenantal participation accruing to their account because of the actions of those for whom they voted. The Old Testament prophets had a phrase for what is happening in many of our nations today. They said to the people, and to the leaders, "You have made a covenant with death." Sometimes God gives us prophetic pictures of the condition of the church. In the year 2,000, the state in which I was born elected a dead man as senator (he died a few weeks prior to the election) but what a prophetic picture. If the church can be swayed by sympathy, we should not be surprised in their choice of a covenant with death through deception or lack of knowledge.

Can you imagine casting a vote for a senator or president of the United States and God putting His finger in your face and saying, "You have made a covenant with death and you will give an account for that covenant of death you made!" Isaiah 28:14-22 says it pretty well:

> *Therefore hear the word of the LORD, you scornful men, Who rule this people who are in the nation's capital, Because you have said,* **"We have made a covenant with death,** *And with Sheol we are in agreement. When the overflowing scourge passes through,* (sounds like New Orleans and Katrina) *It will not come to us, For we have made lies our refuge, And under falsehood we have hidden ourselves." Therefore thus says the LORD God: "Behold, I lay in Zion a stone for a foundation, A tried stone, a precious cornerstone, a sure foundation; Whoever believes will not act hastily. Also I will make justice the measuring line, And righteousness the plummet; The hail will sweep away the refuge of lies, And the waters will overflow the hiding place.* **Your covenant with death** *will be annulled. And your agreement with Sheol will not stand; When the overflowing scourge passes through, Then you will be trampled down by it. As often as it goes out it will take you; For morning by morning it will pass over, And by day and by night; It will be a terror just to understand the report." For the bed is too*

short for a man to stretch out on, And the covering so narrow that he cannot wrap himself in it. For the LORD will rise up as at Mount Perazim, He will be angry as in the Valley of Gibeon—That He may do His work, His awesome work, And bring to pass His act, His unusual act. Now therefore, do not be mockers, Lest your bonds be made strong; For I have heard from the LORD God of hosts, A destruction determined even upon the whole earth.

Have we unknowingly made **covenants with death** because of our votes? Is God demanding repentance before we can see the restoration for which we are so desperately seeking? What kind of acts will God have to perform to annul North America's **covenant with death**? What must happen to the church in order for a realization to dawn that God really does hold us accountable under a system of representative voting? In many cases it seems the church is greatly contributing to filling the land with iniquity by voting for those whose policies demand judgment from on high. Ezekiel saw such a season and prophesied God's response based on these very principles. Ezekiel 9:1-6 states:

Then He called out in my hearing with a loud voice, saying, "Let those who have charge over the city draw near, each with a deadly weapon in his hand." And suddenly six men came from the direction of the upper gate, which faces north, each with his battle-ax in his hand. One man among them was clothed with linen and had a writer's inkhorn at his side. They went in and stood beside the bronze altar. Now the glory of the God of Israel had gone up with the cherub, where it had been, to the threshold of the temple. And He called to the man clothed with linen, who had the writer's inkhorn at his side; and the LORD said to him, "Go through the midst of the city, through the midst of Jerusalem, and put a mark on the foreheads of the men who sigh and cry over all the abominations that are done within it." To the others He said in my hearing, "Go after him through the city and kill; do not let your eye spare, nor have any pity. Utterly slay old and young men, maidens and little children and women; but do not come near anyone on whom is the mark; and begin at

My sanctuary." So they began with the elders who were before the temple.

To qualify for God's mark of protection, one must take an active stance against the designated abominations which bring irreparable judgment to a nation: abortion, witchcraft, drugs and the entire range of sexual sin. The Hebrew word translated "sigh" is **anah** meaning "a deep grief over the condition demanding divine intervention based on a willingness to publicly repent."[12] **Anaq**, the Hebrew word for "cry" has equal depth: "to strangle, to be in anguish, hence used of cries extorted by very great anguish, or sorrow...."[13] The prophet clearly states only those who were grieved at the sin were marked, **leaving those who contributed to the sin suffering judgment**. Do we bear this mark?

There are some who might dismiss this warning by criticizing it as based on an obscure passage hidden in Ezekiel. In Revelation 2:20-21, Jesus said to the church of Thyatira: "Nevertheless I have a few things against you, because you allow that woman Jezebel, who calls herself a prophetess, to teach and beguile My servants to commit sexual immorality and to eat things sacrificed to idols. And I gave her time to repent of her sexual immorality, and she did not repent." "Allow" is the Greek word **eh-ah-o** meaning, "to permit, leave alone, to let alone or refuse to restrain."[14] When the church or its leadership refuses to biblically educate people so they walk unrestrained for fear of losing financial support, then those leaders deserve to hear these words, "Depart from Me you workers of iniquity, I never knew you!"

A demonic serpent's venom has bitten our culture called "tolerance." On college campuses and in government it is dubbed "political correctness," but in the church it is called "tolerance" and once bitten, every victim forfeits divine authority! Jesus rebuked Thyatira for tolerance and they were mild compared to us. For all the modern day Herods who long to silence the church, let the saints arise and pray for them as the early church prayed for Herod with the same results! Jesus guaranteed covenant justice—ask for it! (see *The Sure Mercies of David*).

Revelation 11:18b tells us when Jesus returns to reign, "...And that You should reward Your servants the prophets and the saints, And those who fear Your name, small and great, **And should destroy those who destroy the earth**." Revelation declares Jesus will carry out judgments like what Ezekiel saw. There is nothing obscure about the application of this principle. The fact that Ezekiel saw the judgment beginning at church with its leadership should provide a blinking neon sign concerning the foundational importance of this issue as an elementary qualifier for God's seal.

To sigh and cry over abominations reflects the burden of **intercession** resulting from encountering a culture permeated by actions demanding devastation, destruction and death. It also reflects a refusal to tolerate the growing defilement! Often the church leadership views intercession as a woman's ministry. If this is the case, then according to Ezekiel, only women will be sealed for end-time ministry. If we as church members do not pick up the intercessory prayer burden for our cities, we will not qualify to be marked for end-time service. Ephesians 6 tells us to put on the whole armor of God for the purpose of intercession. Paul preached it from Isaiah 59 where the context is moving God's hand in judgment! The level of intercession in the life of a believer often reflects the condition of the heart, when considering the level of degeneracy in their culture.

One would expect the level of intercession for a Christian living in San Francisco where "same-sex" couples lined up for marriage licenses issued in defiance of state law would vary substantially from one living in Sub-Saharan Africa. Grieving over the sin of our nation reflects a heart in relationship with the Father engaged in heavenly business, and will be rewarded with a mark. Failure to embrace intercession by taking an active position against perversion will forfeit God's end-time mark! Psalm 149 guarantees every saint the honor of executing the written judgment on leaders who pervert the land. See "Jesus & Justice" CD series for the principles guaran-teeing God's intervention when we pray!

How can we as Christians support the deterioration and destruction of our nation by voting for a president and political party boldly championing abortion and homosexual marriage, while attempting to intercede for our nation? In a recent presidential election, one candidate supported abortion and legalized homosexual marriage. Because of what that candidate embraced spiritually, a vote for him was like making a *covenant with death*. When 50 percent of Catholics and 42 percent (according to exit polls) of Protestant Christians, oblivious to the consequences, vote to make a *"covenant with death,"* we have significant numbers in the church scripturally ignorant and grossly unprepared for the last days. We have to ask, what is being preached from our pulpits when 47 percent of those attending religious services once a week think they can establish a *covenant with death* without natural and eternal repercussions? The only encouraging statistic that emerged was for those attending services more than once a week.

Statistical evidence exists proving increased church attendance increases spiritual discernment. Only 35 percent of those attending church more than once a week voted for national judgment by inviting the death covenant. In the strongest way possible, let me emphasize this issue has nothing to do with political affiliation. God is not a member of the Republican, Democrat or Independent parties. If your citizenship is Canadian, God is not explicitly for any one of the four major parties: Liberal, Conservative, Alliance and NDP. Biblical covenantal issues transcend political parties. Adherence to political party over biblical principle is evidence of idolatry.

We are commanded as Christians to extend the Kingdom of God, but a significant percent of our church members are, through deception, extending the kingdom of darkness. Significant judgments will fall upon our respective nations if those of us who have scriptural understanding do not intervene in intercession! The spiritual force of deception is at work incarcerating 84 percent, 55 percent and 42 percent of our major ethnic groups, many of whom attend church, enabling them to blindly "spit in the face" of God's Word? How can the devil deceive 84 percent of an ethnic group into voting for a *covenant with death* by supporting abortion and the homosexual agenda? God's Word surely has answers!

We undoubtedly have believers who vote on Tuesday and attend church on Wednesday praying for the outcome of elections, convinced they have the mind of the Lord. Does God honor spiritual split personality? If we vote for a *covenant with death* on Tuesday and intercede in church on Wednesday until we are blue in the face, God is not moved because of rebellion against His Word. Where did we get the notion God's Word is optional? John, the apostle of love, penned these words in 1 John 2:3-4:

> *Now by this we know that we know Him, if we keep His commandments. He who says, "I know Him," and does not keep His commandments, is a liar, and the truth is not in him.*

When we vote against God's Word, we make ourselves liars and the truth is not in us! How has such dangerous deception overcome so many in the church? Peter speaks about the price of being overcome:

> *...for by whom a person is **overcome**, by him also he is brought into bondage. For if, after they have escaped the pollutions of the world through the knowledge of the Lord and Savior Jesus Christ, they are again entangled in them and overcome, the latter end is worse for them than the beginning. For it would have been better for them not to have known the way of righteousness, than having known it, to turn from the holy commandment delivered to them. But it has happened to them according to the true proverb: "A dog returns to his own vomit," and, "a sow, having washed, to her wallowing in the mire."*

> 2 Peter 2:19-22

Flee vomit—obey God!

Sometimes God uses national events to show the church where people stand spiritually, even though they appear to understand what we preach when attending services. Major segments of Christ's body have little understanding of the covenantal repercussions of the vote, but even more alarming is the absence of "truth through intimacy." We know God intended "truth through intimacy" to be a major seal because He included it in the high priestly prayer of Jesus. John 17:17-23 says:

> *Sanctify them by Your truth. Your word is truth. As you sent Me into the world, I also have sent them into the world. And for their sakes I sanctify Myself, that they also may be sanctified by the truth. I do not pray for these alone, but also*

109

for those who will believe in Me through their word; that
they may all be one, as You, Father, are in Me, and I in you;
that they may also be one in Us, that the world may believe
that You sent Me. And the glory which You gave Me I have
given them, that they may be one just as We are one: I in
them, and You in Me; that they may be made perfect in one,
and that the world may know that You have sent Me, and
have loved them as You have loved Me.

The Song of Solomon 8:6a presents what Jesus prayed in the picture of relationship between bride and Bridegroom: "Set me as a seal upon your heart, As a seal upon your arm...."

When we appropriate the intimacy of relationship pictured here, our arm will only do what we receive in heart-to-heart communication. National elections reveal a significant percentage of the church whose arm is doing what comes from their own head. No one whose heart is sealed could covenant with death. It is incumbent on those of us in leadership positions to take the church into intimacy. We obviously have a ways to go!

National elections also display a cultural political idol where multitudes cast away their Christianity by voting for death and destruction. Perhaps the most plausible answer for believers overlooking biblical standards during elections is in the old adage: everyone votes their pocketbook. If perceived economic concerns are the chief reasons Christians feel free to violate Scripture, then we have identified the idol. It is **mammon**. No wonder Jesus warned we could not serve **GOD** and **mammon**. One possible preparation for receiving Antichrist's mark is living in the deception of voting for death while praying for life. Such actions turn a person's intercession to dung. In Malachi 2:1-3, God spoke to a generation of leaders in parallel circumstances. He called their worship *"dung."* Their covenantal ability to bless people would turn to a curse, meaning all who participated and supported them would share in the judgment. Finally, God promised to spread the dung of their worship on their faces for all to see! Supporting abortion and perversion forfeits God's intercessory mark, making us easy prey for the spirit of Antichrist. Intercession is a call for every church member!

The Root of Bitterness

God demands every believer extend **mercy** and forgiveness because these principles form the foundation of our salvation. When we refuse to honor God's Word in Matthew 18:21-35, we are given over to deception, and through our own judgments become the very essence of what we so vehemently oppose, because the root of bitterness sprouts.

Ministers are leading their followers into covenants of death under the banner of racial equality, feeding them resentment, unforgiveness and bitterness, possibly sealing their future in judgment. Substituting politics and government for God, they attempt to solidify their base by publishing perceived discrimination, while appearing to oppose racism. In truth, racism, unforgiveness and bitterness are the very things they often promote. What they do spiritually is no different than what Jim Jones did physically, in taking his devotees to Guyana and killing them. These leaders will gladly trade the future spiritual fate of their followers in judgment, to establish themselves as national leaders. Masquerading as passionate pastors, they are in fact, more akin to political pimps. 1 Peter 4:17 thunders out a truth:

> For the time has come for judgment to begin at the house of God; and if it begins with us first, what will be the end of those who do not obey the gospel of God?

Jesus overcame racism with love, not political commercials demonstrating the same bitterness He claimed to oppose. When bitterness produces fruit, you become an example of the very thing you hate! Disobeying God's Word individually, corporately, racially and nationally guarantees a demonstration of hypocrisy where we become chief examples of those who commit the very things we condemn. Certain ethnic leaders appear anytime there is even any perceived racial injustice, strongly condemning the apparent perpetrators. The same leaders strongly support the "Dred Scott" decision of our day, "Roe v. Wade" (p. 67). These leaders obviously have impact when the majority of their ethnic group follows their voting recommendation. This dramatic spiritual hypocrisy is astounding! It also forms a foundation for eternal judgment. While claiming to be champions of freedom, they lead people back into a far worse spiritual slavery—bitterness. They started out fighting for a righteous cause, but through years of adversity, apparently unforgiveness became bitterness, tainting and defiling their work. God's heart beats for their deliverance, but very soon the prophets will be invited to the covenant table demanding a leadership transition if repentance and restoration are refused.

I invite you to sow

All you can give,

To lay down your life

That others may live.

CHAPTER 8

Filling Iniquity's Cup

But a certain man named Ananias, with Sapphira his wife, sold a possession. And he kept back part of the proceeds, his wife also being aware of it, and brought a certain part and laid it at the apostles' feet. But Peter said, "Ananias, why has Satan filled your heart to lie to the Holy Spirit and keep back part of the price of the land for yourself? While it remained, was it not your own? And after it was sold, was it not in your control? Why have you conceived this thing in your heart? You have not lied to men but to God." Then Ananias, hearing these words, fell down and breathed his last. So great fear came upon all those who heard these things.

Acts 5:1-5

Fullness not only governs losing or gaining national real estate, but it also governs the life of an individual. Verse 3 says, "...Satan filled (**play-ro-o**)..." Ananias' heart and when his heart became full of iniquity, his body, like the land of Genesis 15, vomited him out. The next question would be, if the enemy can fill an individual or a land, does **fullness** of iniquity also govern transitions in religious systems, cities or regions? Will radical Islam fill a cup of iniquity so that judgment comes? How many innocent people have to die before the church demands divine justice upon the demonized? The ultimate justice would be losing their people to Christianity. Matthew 23:13-15 speaks to the issue:

> *But woe to you, scribes and Pharisees, hypocrites! For you shut up the kingdom of heaven against men; for you neither go in yourselves, nor do you allow those who are entering to go in. Woe to you, scribes and Pharisees, hypocrites! For you devour widows' houses, and for a pretense make long prayers. Therefore you will receive greater condemnation. Woe to you, scribes and Pharisees, hypocrites! For you travel land and sea to win one proselyte, and when he is won, you make him twice as much a son of hell as yourselves.*

Freedom of religion was never intended to allow treasonous terrorists' training camps masquerading as mosques! It is time to terrorize the terrorists!

Verses 25-28 continue:

> *Woe to you, scribes and Pharisees, hypocrites! For you cleanse the **outside** of the cup and dish, but **inside** they are **full** of extortion and self-indulgence. Blind Pharisee, first cleanse the **inside** of the cup and dish, that the **outside** of them may be clean also. Woe to you, scribes and Pharisees, hypocrites! For you are like whitewashed tombs which indeed appear beautiful **outwardly**, but **inside** are **full** of dead men's bones and all uncleanness. Even so you also outwardly appear righteous to men, but inside you are full of hypocrisy and lawlessness.*

Matthew 23 portrays Jesus declaring **fullness** of iniquity over the religious system, based on the fact that its leaders corrupted its ordinances, ultimately rejecting the very One they claimed to represent. The radical Islamists claim to be the ones who best represent Islam's core values. Is it any wonder the Jesus of Revelation judges and makes war? Do we know Him? Are we prepared to represent Him in judging and making war? The choices men make lead to being full of God or full of demons. Whose marks will we take? This is a perfect picture of what happens to unmarked believers at the end of the age. Verses 32-36 finish the judgment but seem to contradict a principle of Ezekiel 16.

Fill up, then, the measure of your father's guilt. Serpents, brood of vipers! How can you escape the condemnation of hell? Therefore, indeed, I send you prophets, wise men, and scribes: some of them you will kill and crucify, and some of them you will scourge in your synagogues and persecute from city to city, that on you may come all the righteous blood shed on the earth, from the blood of righteous Abel to the blood of Zechariah, son of Berechiah, whom you murdered between the temple and the altar. Assuredly, I say to you, all these things will come upon this generation.

In Ezekiel 16, God says He will not hold one man accountable for another man's sin. But here we see Jesus holding the generation of His visitation accountable for previous generations' rejections. He told them in verse 35 that on them would:

...come all the righteous blood shed on the earth, from the blood of righteous Abel to the blood of Zechariah, son of Berechiah, whom was murdered between the temple and the altar.

Verse 36 is definitive when Jesus says, "Assuredly, I say to you, all these things will come upon this generation." Our question then is why did everything seem to fall in judgment on that generation? The answer has to be found in verse 32 where Jesus said, "Fill up (**play-ro-so-te**), then, the measure of your fathers' guilt." In rejecting the very One they claimed to represent, the religious system filled the cup of iniquity and they were vomited out. Their house, so to speak, spewed them out like the land of Leviticus 20 and the bodies of Ananias and Sapphira. In verse 38 of Matthew 23 Jesus said, "See! Your house is left to you desolate...." The result was God instituting a new religious system. A new covenant was born. God redefined and broadened what it meant to be Israel and redefined what it meant to be a Jew (of Jew and Gentile He made **one new man**).

We note from 2 Corinthians 11:1-4:

Oh, that you would bear with me in a little folly—and indeed you do bear with me. For I am jealous for you with godly jealousy. For I have betrothed you to one husband, that I may present you as a chaste virgin to Christ. But I fear, lest somehow, as the serpent deceived Eve by his craftiness, so your minds may be corrupted from the simplicity that is in Christ. For if he who comes preaches another Jesus whom we have not preached, or if you receive a different spirit which you have not received, or a different gospel which you have not accepted, you may well put up with it.

In 2 Peter 2:1-3, we see the enemy immediately attempting to corrupt this new covenant with counterfeits:

But there were also false prophets among the people, even as there will be false teachers among you, who will secretly bring in destructive heresies, even denying the Lord who bought them, and bring on themselves swift destruction. And many will follow their destructive ways because of whom the way of truth will be blasphemed. By **covetousness** (mammon's mistress), *they will exploit you with deceptive words; for a long time their judgment has not been idle, and their destruction does not slumber.*

It is interesting to look at the counterfeit today in the personage of Islam and the cults, which all have one thing in common. They preach a salvation that denies the blood of Jesus as the foundation for redemption, while shunning the concepts of embracing the cross in the life of the believer, substituting pharisaical rules and regulations in its place. While a cancerous assault continues on biblical credibility, the church faces the potential of its finest hour through preparation and possessing fullness of Christ.

Birthing a New Heavens and Earth

If we have been promised a new heavens and a new earth, what is the price tag for bringing the promise into existence? The book of Revelation clearly presents the concept of fullness governing the transition from the old heavens and earth to the new heavens and earth, with each opposing group marked by their God of choice! Does the old earth have to be filled with iniquity before we get to inherit a new one? If so, what or who fills the cup?

Revelation 17:1-5 says:

*Then one of the seven angels who had the seven bowls came and talked with me, saying to me, "Come, I will show you the judgment of the great harlot who sits on many waters, with whom the kings of the earth committed fornication, and the inhabitants of the earth were made drunk with the wine of her fornication," So he carried me away in the Spirit into the wilderness. And I saw a woman sitting on a scarlet beast which was **full** of names of blasphemy, having seven heads and ten horns. The woman was arrayed in purple and scarlet, and adorned with gold and precious stones and pearls, having in her hand a golden cup **full** of abominations and the filthiness of her fornication.*

And on her forehead a name was written:
MYSTERY, BABYLON THE GREAT, THE MOTHER OF HARLOTS AND OF THE ABOMINATIONS OF THE EARTH.

Revelation 17 reveals the counterfeit church **fills** the cup in the last days. One might wonder how they will accomplish this feat. Verses 13 and 14 of chapter 17 say:

These are of one mind, and they will give their power and authority to the beast. These will make war with the Lamb, and the Lamb will overcome them, for He is Lord of lords and King of kings; and those who are with Him are called, chosen, and faithful.

In Revelation 19, we get a picture of Jesus descending from heaven. Revelation 19:11-16 says:

Then I saw heaven opened, and behold, a white horse. And He who sat on him was called Faithful and True, and in righteousness He judges and makes war. His eyes were like a flame of fire, and on His head were many crowns. He had a name written that no one knew except Himself. He was clothed with a robe dipped in blood, and His name is called The Word of God. And the armies in heaven, clothed in fine linen, white and clean, followed Him on white horses. Now out of His mouth goes a sharp sword, that with it He should strike the nations. And He Himself will rule them with a

*rod of iron. He Himself treads the winepress of the fierceness
and wrath of Almighty God. And He has on His robe and
on His thigh a name written KING OF KINGS AND
LORD OF LORDS.*

Now the question should be, "What is it that brings Jesus out of
heaven with His army?" The very thing that brings Jesus out of
heaven is revealed in Revelation 19:1-2:

*After these things I heard a loud voice of a great multitude
in heaven, saying, "Alleluia! Salvation and glory and honor
and power to the Lord our God! For true and righteous are
His judgments, because He has judged the great harlot who
corrupted the earth with her fornication; and He has
avenged on her the blood of His **servants shed by her.**"*

Just as the religious system of Jesus' day claimed to represent God
while crucifying Immanuel in their midst, so in the last days a
counterfeit religious system destroys and kills the real Christians in
their midst (Islam qualifies). This action fills the cup, making a new
heavens and earth possible. The answer to the question of what it
costs to birth a new heavens and a new earth has a very simple
answer: **your blood and mine**. In Revelation 17, we quoted verses
1-5, but verse 6 says:

*And I saw the woman, drunk with the **blood of the saints**
and with the **blood of the martyrs of Jesus**. And when I
saw her I marveled with great amazement."*

It is the **blood of the saints** that fills the cup and births a new
heavens and earth. Revelation 6:9-11 says it best:

*When He opened the fifth seal, I saw under the altar the
souls of those who had been slain for the word of God and for
the testimony which they held. And they cried with a loud
voice, saying, "How long, O Lord, holy and true, until You
judge and **avenge our blood** on those who dwell on the
earth?" And a white robe was given to each of them; and it
was said to them that they should rest a little while longer,
until both the number of their fellow servants and their
brethren, who would be killed as they were, was **completed**
[play-ro-o].*

The Greek word for *"completed"* in verse 11 is **play-ro-o** and it takes us back to Matthew 23:32 where Jesus said, "**Play-ro-so-te** the measure of your fathers' guilt." The book of Revelation clearly reveals that the cost of birthing a new heavens and a new earth is **fullness.** Jesus is our pattern. Just as His martyrdom filled the cup of the Old Testament, demanding a transition and birthing a new covenant, the church's martyrdom fills the cup of the old earth, demanding a transition birthing a new heavens and a new earth. The martyrdom of the saints is what fills the cup. Many were in denial about the holocaust as it was transpiring. We need to ask ourselves if another **holocaust** is happening now. For the Christians in some Muslim nations it is already here. Radical Islam promises the justification for wholesale murder of Christians and Jews. In Revelation 16:4, we are told the rivers and springs of water become blood. Verse 6 reveals, "For they have shed the blood of saints and prophets, And You have given them blood to drink."

How many more Darfurs will we have before God releases such a judgment? As radical Islam overcomes more nations, this prophecy of Revelation becomes very real. Revelation judgments will manifest. It seems denial is the only way to overlook the implications of the text, but there may be enough denial working currently in the church to last for many years. There is no other way to birth a new heavens and a new earth. What if our pervasive seeker-sensitive preaching becomes gross spiritual negligence (but sells well), denying future generations the preparation so desperately needed to bravely face filling the cup?

Is there any preparation in your church for martyrdom? More expect the rapture than expect to be martyred! 1 Thessalonians 4:17 says we will have a catching away, and we will, but that does not nullify the principle of **fullness.** Understanding **fullness** changes the focus on the rapture equation. The real issue is not how much of God's wrath will the church be present to observe (pre-trib, mid or post), but how much of man's Christ-rejecting wrath can the church take in "**filling** the cup" and birthing a "new heavens and earth." God's wrath is quite separate and distinct from man's wrath. The book of Revelation shows God's wrath as a divine, though often delayed, response to man's wrath. Just as God used man's wrath against Jesus to birth salvation, He uses man's wrath against the end-time church to produce a new heavens and earth. The more we play with seeker-sensitivity the less the church is prepared to pay the price to fill the cup. Rapture blurs the line between God's wrath and man's wrath, confusing the real **issue—fullness**. Are we preparing a generation to pay the "fullness" price? There is only one wise course of action: prepare for persecution by developing Daniel's mentality.

We have had decades of "prophetic preachers" proclaiming the soon return and catching away of the church quoting Daniel's "70th week." Ironically, it is the book of Daniel which strongly reveals and supports the principle of fullness governing this end-time transition. Daniel 8:23-24 says:

> *And in the latter time of their kingdom, When the transgressors have reached their* **"fullness,"** *A king shall arise, Having fierce features, Who understands sinister schemes. His power shall be mighty, but not by his own power; He shall destroy fearfully, And shall prosper and thrive; He shall destroy the mighty, and also the* **holy people***.*

Daniel prophesied the same thing John saw and declared in Revelation. Daniel knew what it was like to have leaders seeking his death and destruction. He walked in a place with God where lions could not kill him and jealous leaders could not displace him. Our challenge is to raise a generation who walk with Daniel's commitment and divine protection!

Marking Believers for a Second Holocaust?

Many, since World War II, have found it very difficult to understand why God would have allowed a holocaust devastating the Jewish people. God may not cause most of the great devastations in the earth, but He is usually there to redeem them. We can surely all agree concerning God's great redemption of the holocaust in fulfilling Isaiah's prophetic proclamation, "Shall a nation be born in a day?" The immediate postwar political realities were such that, without the sympathy generated by the holocaust, Israel as a nation could never have been born in a single day.

Isaiah 66:5-10 says:

> *Hear the word of the LORD, You who tremble at His word: "Your brethren who hated you, Who cast you out for My name's sake, said, 'Let the LORD be glorified, That we may see your joy.' But they shall be ashamed." The sound of noise from the city! A voice from the temple! The voice of the LORD, Who fully repays His enemies! "Before she travailed, she gave birth; Before her pain came, She delivered a male child. Who has heard such a thing? Who has seen such things? Shall the earth be made to give birth in one day? Or shall a nation be born at once? For as soon as **Zion travailed,** She gave birth to her children. Shall I bring to the time of birth, and not cause delivery?" says the LORD. "Shall I who cause delivery shut up the womb?" says your God. "Rejoice...."*

It took a holocaust to birth the nation of Israel, and God said rejoice. The God of all creation saw man's ethnic hatred and rebellion then redeemed it by fulfilling His promised prophetic blessing. Only a holocaust moved the nations to vote in Jerusalem's favor. The nation of Israel exists for mainly two reasons. The first, to fulfill prophetic promise, and second, to be grafted in by the church. God will redeem their holocaust, possibly when they recognize the church marching through the same thing with a far different grace and glory on their lives, thus making the Jew jealous.

What if the end-time church while enduring sporadic holocaust persecutions also rises to a level of faith where they represent Jesus the Judge and bring God's justice manifesting the Messiah of the prophets? The Jews have been looking for the Judge of all the earth for over 2,000 years. What better time to reveal Him than in sporadic holocaust conditions. Muslim political leaders have declared their plan of developing nuclear weapons to destroy Israel. God promises in Romans 11 to save Israel. What is the church to do with this obvious conflict? When Paul faced Elymas, he moved God's hand upon him with blindness. When the early church faced a Herod bent on destroying their leaders—they prayed—God answered with an angel of judgment. We should do the same (to learn how, see "Jesus & Justice" CD series). The book of Revelation portrays man's final great rebellion and hatred manifested toward believers, with the promise of redemption. God's prophetic plan to graft Israel back into the tree and fill the cup, bringing a new heavens and a new earth, apparently comes in one final, extended season. Even with all this resistance, we are promised nations. The church pays the price to fill the cup. The church pays the price to fulfill prophetic promise. The New Testament says first the natural and then the spiritual. As it was with natural Israel, so must it be with spiritual Israel. Should that scare us or excite us?

I learned about fear from personal experience before making Jesus "LORD." My Navy logbook says I flew 161 combat missions in Vietnam, but I only remember 135. On several occasions, Migs attempted to intercept and destroy our reconnaissance airplane. When hours of routine boredom suddenly turned into ten minutes of panic, two very visible and dramatically different groupings of men emerged. One group had already made their decision, "this war is worth the sacrifice of our lives," while the other was somewhere in "limbo land" having yet to make any real decision. Those who chose to sow their life for the cause were functioning without the paralysis of fear, empowered to do what was necessary to save lives. Those who had not made the decision to give their life were literally "locked up," and looked as if they were swimming in molasses. The value of personal commitment became clear in that season, with a $35 million dollar plane and 30 men hanging in the balance. Fear is the spiritual heritage of the unprepared. Fear will be eclipsed by faith if we embrace the covenant promises that accompany such an impending season!

Daniel 9:24 says:

> *Seventy weeks are determined for your people and for your holy city, to finish the transgression, to make an end of sins, to make reconciliation for iniquity, to bring in everlasting righteousness, to seal up vision and prophecy, and to anoint the Most Holy.*

To "...finish the transgression..." could easily be translated "to bring to **fullness**." The problem with the rapture doctrine, as it has been taught through the decades, is it gives us all the blessing of eternity with no cost or price tag. It reflects a very cheap gospel. Inevitably, when generations embrace the rapture, they stop preparing the succeeding generation to walk with God. The rapture as currently preached, is rooted in a cheap salvation, and completely denies the divine principle of **fullness**. How will a generation fed little but seeker-sensitivity and rapture, respond if persecution comes instead? Does milk-toast and mush prepare the church to be available to fill the cup, to birth a new heavens and a new earth? The answer is obvious. Preparing is the wisest thing to do. The book of Revelation describes another holocaust coming! Evidence exists that it is here! We have a generation desperately desiring the power of the early church without making the same level of commitment and without walking through God's open door. When we read excerpts of what the early church leaders preached, we discover they repeatedly sought personally the same pattern Jesus established. They refused to be cheated.

Jesus spent a significant amount of time preparing the Twelve to follow the pattern He would soon establish. Jesus knew the earth's cup would have to be filled, and He set the prophetic stage by including a call to martyrdom in preparing the Twelve. In Matthew 10, Jesus spent half of His instruction outlining the commitment to martyrdom necessary for service. Matthew 10:17-39 says:

> *But beware of men, for they will deliver you up to councils and scourge you in their synagogues. And you will be brought before governors and kings for My sake, as a testimony to them and to the Gentiles. But when they deliver you up, do not worry about how or what you should speak. For it will be given to you in that hour what you should speak; for it is not you who speak, but the Spirit of your Father who speaks in you. Now brother will deliver up brother to death, and a father his child; and children will rise up against parents and cause them to be put to death. And you will be hated by all for My name's sake. But he who endures to the end will be saved. But when they persecute you in this city, flee to another. For assuredly, I say to you, you will not have gone through the cities of Israel before the Son of Man comes.*

A disciple is not above his teacher, nor a servant above his master.

It is enough for a disciple that he be like his teacher, and a servant like his master. If they have called the master of the house Beelzebub, how much more will they call those of his household! Therefore do not fear them. For there is nothing covered that will not be revealed, and hidden that will not be known. Whatever I tell you in the dark, speak in the light; and what you hear in the ear, preach on the housetops. And do not fear those who kill the body but cannot kill the soul. But rather fear Him who is able to destroy both soul and body in hell.

Are not two sparrows sold for a copper coin? And not one of them falls to the ground apart from your Father's will. But the very hairs of your head are all numbered. Do not fear therefore; you are of more value than many sparrows. Therefore whoever confesses Me before men, him I will also confess before My Father who is in heaven. But whoever denies Me before men, him I will also deny before My Father who is in heaven. Do not think that I came to bring peace on earth. I did not come to bring peace but a sword. For I have come to set a man against his father, a daughter against her mother, and a daughter-in-law against her mother-in-law. And a man's foes will be those of his own household. He who loves father or mother more than Me is not worthy of Me. And he who loves son or daughter more than Me is not worthy of Me. And he who does not take his cross and follow after Me is not worthy of Me. He who finds his life will lose it, and he who loses his life for My sake will find it.

The power demonstrated in Jesus' ministry and possessed by the early church in the book of Acts had a strong relational component. They were expected to make the same commitment Jesus made. They were not their own! They had been bought with a price, and God demanded the right to sow each life into His eternal purposes.

What the Early Church Taught

The magnitude of what Jesus taught as essential commitment to the Christian experience can be seen in church history even in the second and third century. When looking for a representative church father of the second century, the crucial nature of the subject matter necessitates that it be a stable, proven and notable voice. The individual chosen has made an enormous contribution to the church extending even to the present day. His work has been credited as the foundation upon which, "Cyprian and Augustine built up, with incomparable genius, that Carthaginian School of Christian thought by which Latin Theology was dominated for centuries."[15] This in turn through Augustine fueled the Reformation in Germany and Continental Europe. It has been said the specialties of the Anglican Reformation were in like proportion, due to the writings of this man and his chief disciple. He lived from 145 to 220 AD holding positions as Presbyter in both Carthage and Rome. He was first to coin the phrase "Trinity" and define it. He defined Christian views on marriage. His name was Quintus Septimeus Florens Tertuleanus, or just Tertullian. He wrote a piece entitled *Scorpiace*, in which he stated,

> *"But if, for the contest's sake, God had appointed martyrdoms for us, that thereby we might make trial with our opponent, in order that He may now keep bruising him by whom man chose to be bruised, here too generosity rather than harshness in God holds sway. For He wished to make man, now plucked from the devil's throat by faith, trample upon him likewise by courage, that he might not merely have escaped from, but also completely vanquished, his enemy.*[16]

The early church believed we fully conquered Satan by refusing to deny Christ unto death. They sought this experience. They felt cheated if they were not martyred.

The Octavius by Minucius Felix records an argument between unbelieving Caecilius and the Christian Octavius. The real issue here is the content demonstrating the prevalent view of martyrdom as a privilege to be sought. Minucius writes:

(1) *"How beautiful is the spectacle to God when A Christian does battle with pain; when he is drawn up against threats, and punishments, and tortures; when, mocking the noise of death, he treads underfoot the horror of the executioner; when he raises up his liberty against kings and princes, and yields to God alone, whose he is; when, triumphant and victorious, he tramples upon the very man who has pronounced sentence against him! For he has conquered who has obtained that for which he contends."*[17]

Jerome mentions Minucius as an advocate in Rome prior to his conversion. Octavius appears to have been written about 166 AD and provides a good glimpse of the second century church.

For the final snapshot of how the early church viewed martyrdom, we turn to the third century and a writer whose **"heart theology"** was formed by what happened in Antioch. His name was Thascius Caecilius Cypranus, or Cyprian, and he became Bishop of Carthage. He was an exceptionally authoritative voice on this subject, not just because he was Tertullian's spiritual son, but because he experienced martyrdom at the hands of Emperor Velarian in 257. The faithfulness of the Holy Spirit prepared Cyprian. The same Holy Spirit is attempting to prepare the next generation. Do we have ears to hear? Cyprian records this exchange:

(2) *"Therefore, again, we say, brother Cyprian, we have received great joy, great comfort, great refreshment, especially in that you have described, with glorious and deserved praises, the glorious, I will not say, deaths, but immortalities of martyrs. For such departures should have been proclaimed with such words, that the · things which were related might be told in such manner as they were done. Thus, from your letter, we saw those glorious triumphs of the martyrs; and with our eyes in some sort have followed them as they went to heaven, and have contemplated them seated among angels, and the powers and dominions of heaven. Moreover, we have in some manner perceived with our ears the Lord giving them the promised testimony in the presence of the Father. It is this, then, which also raises our spirit day by day, and inflames us to the following of the track of such dignity.*

(3) ***"For what more glorious, or what more blessed, can happen to any man from the divine condescension, than to***: *confess the Lord God, in death itself, before his very executioners; Than among the raging and varied and exquisite tortures of worldly power, even when the body is racked and torn and cut to pieces to confess Christ the Son of God with a spirit still free, although departing; Than to have mounted to heaven with the world left behind; Than, having forsaken men, to stand among the angels; Than, all worldly impediments being broken through, already to stand free in the sight of God; Than to enjoy the heavenly kingdom without any delay; Than to have become an associate of Christ's passion in Christ's name; Than to have become by the divine condescension the judge of one's own judge; Than to have brought off an unstained conscience from the confession of His name; Than to have refused to obey human and sacrilegious laws against the faith; Than to have borne witness to the truth with a public testimony; Than, by dying, to have subdued death itself, which is dreaded by all; Than, by death itself, to have attained immortality; Than when torn to pieces, and tortured by all the instruments of cruelty, to have overcome the torture by the tortures themselves; Than by strength of mind to have wrestled with all the agonies of a mangled body? Than not to have shuddered at the flow of one's own blood; Than to have begun to love one's punishments, after having faith to bear them; (Supplicia sua post fidem amare carpiss); Than to think it an injury to one's life not to have left it?*

(4) *"For to this battle our Lord, as with the trumpet of His Gospel, stimulates us when He says, 'He that loveth father or mother more than me is not worthy of me: and he that loveth his own soul more than me is not worthy of me. And he that taketh not his cross, and followeth after me, is not worthy of me.' (Matthew x.37,38). And again, 'Blessed are they which are persecuted for righteousness' sake: for theirs is the kingdom of heaven. Blessed shall ye be, when men shall persecute you, and hate you. Rejoice, and be exceeding glad: for so did their fathers persecute the prophets which were before you." (Matthew v.10-12). And again, 'Because ye shall stand before kings and powers, and the brother shall deliver up the brother to death, and the father the son, and he that endureth to the end shall be saved;' (Matthew x.18, xxi.22) and 'To him that over-cometh will*

I give to sit on my throne, even as I also overcame and am set down on the throne of my Father.' (Revelation iii.21). Moreover the apostle: 'Who shall separate us from the love of Christ? Shall tribulation, or distress, or persecution, or famine, or nakedness, or peril, or sword? (As it is written, For thy sake are we killed all the day long; we are accounted as sheep for the slaughter.) Nay, in all these things we are more than conquerors for Him who hath loved us.' (Romans viii.35).

(5) "*When we read these things, [Footnote:* **Note the power of the Holy Scripture in creating and supporting the martyr-spirit.***] and things of the like kind, brought together in the Gospel, and feel, as it were, torches placed under us, with the Lord's words to inflame our faith, we not only do not dread, but we even provoke the enemies of the truth; and we have already conquered the opponents of God, by the very fact of our not yielding to them, and have subdued their* **nefarious laws against the truth.** *And although we have not yet shed our blood, we are prepared to shed it. Let no one think that this delay of our departure (Lit. "of our postponement.") is any clemency; for it obstructs us, it makes a hindrance to our glory, it puts off heaven, it withholds the glorious sight of God. For in a contest of this kind, and in the kind of contest when faith is struggling in the encounter, it is not true clemency to put off martyrs by delay. Entreat therefore, beloved Cyprian, that of His mercy the Lord will every day more and more arm and adorn every one of us with greater abundance and readiness, and will confirm and strengthen us by the strength of His power; and, as a good captain, will at length bring forth His soldiers, whom He has hitherto trained and proved in the camp of our prison, to the field of the battle set before them. May He hold forth to us the divine arms, those weapons that know not how to be conquered, — the breastplate of righteousness, which is never accustomed to be broken, — the shield of faith, which cannot be pierced through, — the helmet of salvation, which cannot be shattered, — and the sword of the Spirit, which has never been wont to be injured. For to whom should we rather commit these things for him to ask for us, than to our so reverend bishop, [I have amended the translation here from the Oxford trans] as destined victims asking help of the priests?*"[18]

The heart of the early church is revealed through their words. Their hearts cried to God, **"For what more glorious, or what more blessed, can happen to any man from (God) than**: to confess the Lord God, in death itself, before his very executioners, to think it an injury to one's life not to have left it?" Compare the early church which cried to God for martyrdom, so they would not be cheated eternally, with today's church which cries not to be cheated out of the rapture! What is wrong with this picture? What words could a minister muster if called to account by the Master for not preparing his flock for martyrdom because through seeker-sensitivity he wanted a successful church? Success in the natural can guarantee failure eternally!

Fullness and the Harvest

Perhaps this is a glimpse of why there will be silence in heaven for half an hour. Much of the ministry will be in shock trying to recover (Revelation 8:1).

Romans 11 gives us a panoramic view of a monumental harvest still facing the church before we can even consider the rapture and conclusion of this age. God says of this latter season concerning Israel and the church in Romans 11:11-15 and 25-36:

> *I say then, have they stumbled that they should fall? Certainly not! But through their fall, to provoke them to jealousy, salvation has come to the Gentiles. Now if their fall is riches for the world, and their failure riches for the Gentiles, how much more their **fullness**! For I speak to you Gentiles; inasmuch as I am an apostle to the Gentiles, I magnify my ministry, if by any means I may provoke to jealousy those who are my flesh and save some of them. For if their being cast away is the reconciling of the world, what will their acceptance be but life from the dead? For I do not desire, brethren, that you should be ignorant of this mystery, lest you should be wise in your own opinion, that hardening in part has happened to Israel until the **fullness** of the Gentiles has come in. And so all Israel will be saved, as it is written: The Deliverer will come out of Zion, And He will turn away ungodliness from Jacob; For this is My covenant*

with them, When I take away their sins' Concerning the gospel they are enemies for your sake, but concerning the election they are beloved for the sake of the fathers. For the gifts and the calling of God are irrevocable. For as you were once disobedient to God, yet have now obtained mercy through their disobedience, even so these also have now been disobedient, that through the mercy shown you they also may obtain mercy. For God has committed them all to disobedience, that He might have mercy on all. Oh, the depth of the riches both of the wisdom and knowledge of God! How unsearchable are His judgments and His ways past finding out! For who has known the mind of the LORD? Or who has become His counselor? Or who has first given to Him And it shall be repaid to him? For of Him and through Him and to Him are all things, to whom be glory forever. Amen.

Just like **play-ro-mah** governs the winding up of the age and is the key issue in birthing a new heavens and a new earth, so does **play-ro-mah** govern the harvest. Fullness is a qualifying issue. The principle dictates we do not qualify for God's fullness for the harvest until we place the seed of our life in His care, willing to be planted at His direction, contributing to fullness in the earth when and where Father desires. Psalm 2:8 says:

Ask of Me, and I will give You The nations for Your inheritance, And the ends of the earth for Your possession.

Verse 9 says:

You shall break them with a rod of iron; You shall dash them in pieces like a potter's vessel.

The church is charged with harvesting the nations according to Romans 11:25:

*For I do not desire, brethren, that you should be ignorant of this mystery, lest you should be wise in your own opinion, that hardening in part has happened to Israel until the **fullness** of the Gentiles has come in.*

Psalm 2:8 reaches fulfillment in the church as we move into the end-times, and immediately following the actualization of Romans 11:25, Romans 11:12 rises to demand recognition:

> *Now if their fall is riches for the world, and their failure riches for the Gentiles, how much more their **fullness**!*

Verse 26 puts it this way:

> *And so all Israel will be saved, as it is written: "The Deliverer will come out of Zion, And He will turn away ungodliness from Jacob; For this is My covenant with them, When I take away their sins."*

Romans 11 makes it very clear that the church has to reach **play-ro-mah** over cities and nations, impacting them for the kingdom. Then and only then can we move toward **play-ro-mah** for the Jewish nation. If we seriously consider these assignments and the magnitude of mobilization necessary to fulfill such a call, how could we ever contemplate the Lord's return to take us out of here, when the majority of the harvest is still standing in the field? When we look at the magnitude of the harvest assigned to the church, we realize we could easily have two or three more decades to complete the necessary work.

Play-ro-mah governs the Gentile harvest. **Play-ro-mah** governs the Jewish harvest. **Play-ro-mah** governs birthing a new heavens and a new earth. **Play-ro-mah** is a governmental word, the key to end-time release of Father's heart and the advancement of the church.

History is threatening to continue repeating itself as radical Islamists prepare to launch even greater holocaust manifestations on both Jews and Christians. The values of Islam are on display for all who dare to look and see. Wherever Radical Imams hold sway over government leaders, destruction and death follow. We have little choice but to prepare a generation for war. Christians are going to have to fight for their neighborhoods and nation.

What would we say if God's pathway for grafting the Jewish nation back into the olive tree was through such an intense conflict that it demanded judgments of biblical proportions? Millions of dollars have been contributed by Jewish people to organizations formed for the very purpose of raising the battle cry of the modern Jewish citizen, "Never Again," referring to the devastations endured in Europe during Word War II. But a conflict of equal intensity is being waged from nation to nation. Islamists, resembling Hitler in their tactics, are battling for nations with one goal—world domination. The church is being forced to respond or forfeit a promised harvest. Are we preparing a generation to move God's hand in judgment? (Read *The Sure Mercies of David* for an introduction.)

In Revelation 3:8, Jesus said to the church of Philadelphia:

> *I know your works. See, I have set before you an open door, and no one can shut it; for you have a little strength, have kept My word, and have not denied My name.*

One question needs to be answered by leaders: Are we pursuing success with an unintended consequence of placing a whole Christian generation in jeopardy of "denying Jesus" through lack of preparation? What will multitudes do when faced with, "bow or burn?" As church leaders and teachers who will receive stricter judgments, we must refuse to be responsible for not preparing a generation.

The choice to let God spend us as change in His pocket, whether filling the cup and bringing forth a new heavens and a new earth or accepting a missionary call must be made by every believer! Not leading the church into such commitments denies scripture, denies the pattern Jesus lived and denies the example of the early church. Is the church today living in denial? We have taught Jesus as Savior, but have we taught Jesus as **LORD**? Yielding all to God is our reasonable worship. It is an open door to a dimension and level in the Spirit where exceedingly great and precious promises begin to manifest in our behalf. When we make the commitment to let God take our life and spend it however He wills, we walk through a doorway in the realm of the Spirit to a place of qualification for the **play-ro-mah** (fullness) of God for an end-time harvest.

Revelation 22:10-11 says:

> *And he said to me, "Do not seal the words of the prophecy of this book, for the time is at hand. He who is unjust, let him*

be unjust still; he who is filthy, let him be filthy still; he who is righteous, let him be righteous still; he who is holy, let him be holy still."

Verse 11 presents us a picture of two groups on a parallel growth plan moving toward cataclysmic confrontation. The word *"still"* comes from the Greek word **eti** and here denotes the development and crystallization of character. Verse 11 paints a picture of two opposing forces, each one progressively growing more and more like the God whom they choose to worship. This progressive discipleship brings ultimate fulfillment, dramatized by the encounter of Cain and Abel. Throughout the history of man, the greatest and most cruel persecution of true religion has always come from false or counterfeit religion. The story of Cain and Abel is the first picture of these two forces interacting. Abel represents obedience to a higher plan, faith in God, the need for a sacrifice, the necessity of the shedding of blood, and the supernatural power of God manifested through obedience. Cain, on the other hand, represents human religion, good works, without the shed blood, without a substitutionary sacrifice, offering the fruit of an earth already cursed by God. Both true and counterfeit produce fruit. The fruit of these two systems are reflected by the end product in character and nature of what they produce. Paul commented on this fruit in Philippians 2:20-21:

For I have no one like-minded, who will sincerely care for your state. For all seek their own, not the things which are of Christ Jesus.

And also Philippians 3:17-19:

Brethren, join in following my example, and note those who so walk, as you have us for a pattern. For many walk, of whom I have told you often, and now tell you even weeping, that they are the enemies of the cross of Christ: whose end is destruction, whose god is their belly, and whose glory is in their shame—who set their mind on earthly things.

If we refuse the cross, selfishness will prevail and defile our future in God. Some would argue, "This is too much adversity for any in the succeeding generation to accept." Only when we open our hearts to understand the preparational power of the mark of adversity, can we receive the Father's heart. Job 31:35-37 states:

> *Oh, that I had one to hear me! Here is my mark. Oh, that the Almighty would answer me, That my Prosecutor had written a book! Surely I would carry it on my shoulder, And bind it on me like a crown; I would declare to Him the number of my steps; Like a prince I would approach Him.*

Job wanted covenant relationship with God where his prayers were answered, where he could decree a thing and God would establish it! All the devastation produced a single mark. It is the mark of the prophets and must be birthed by adversity. 1 Samuel 3:19-20 says:

> *So Samuel grew, and the LORD was with him and let none of his words fall to the ground. And all Israel from Dan to Beersheba knew that Samuel had been established as a prophet of the LORD.*

Hannah birthed Samuel's anointing through adversity. Not one word fell to the ground because God initiated the action. Adversity brings us to the end of ourselves where God can initiate all the action. Job recognized God's mark and proclaimed it. We can run from adversity or run toward it. Embracing the cross means running toward adversity, while rejecting it jeopardizes receiving the necessary mark. In the last days, we will be like the religious system to which we adhere. There are no other options. Abel's religion produced a martyr. Cain's religion produced a murderer. Revelation 22:11 indicates we will either be in one camp or the other. The question is, "Which one?"

A fearful time will

Some day come,

The martyrs lay down

One by one.

These deaths for all

The world to see,

The fullness of

Iniquity.

CHAPTER 9

Fullness of God

It seems the counterfeit almost always precedes the real. This demands a greater measure of the Father's discernment, and manifesting it as a matter of survival. As Satan continues to capture and fill individuals with an ever-increasing passion for perversion, the church must rise to the confrontation by possessing the marks of God. Colossians 1:15-20 brings a statement that hardly anyone in the church has a problem with. We can all easily agree with this passage:

> *He is the image of the invisible God, the firstborn over all creation. For by Him all things were created that are in heaven and that are on earth, visible and invisible, whether thrones or dominions or principalities or powers. All things were created through Him and for Him. And He is before all things, and in Him all things consist. And He is the head of the body, the church, who is the beginning, the firstborn from the dead, that in all things He may have the preeminence. For it pleased the Father that in Him all the **fullness** should dwell, and by Him to reconcile all things to Himself, by Him, whether things on earth or things in heaven, having made peace through the blood of His cross. For it pleased the Father that in Him all the **fullness** should dwell....*

Everyone agrees the fullness of the Godhead was resident in Jesus. But there is a progression in this passage easily overlooked, as it continues through chapter 1 on into chapter 2. The historical context needs to be considered for understanding, but should not overshadow the spiritual truth of the passage. Gnosticism became a heresy the early fathers fought because it separated matter (your physical body) from thought (what you believed). The Gnostics taught you could do anything with your body (sex, drugs, whatever) as long as what you believed was right (the original version of situational ethics). This resulted in separating the physical body from the spirit—freeing the body to do whatever seemed good. Purity was a function of the spirit, allowing the physical body to indulge every fleshly desire. Reaction to the excesses of this doctrine led ultimately to asceticism, which became the core of the monastic movement. While Paul clearly addresses these issues, a still permeating truth rises from these chapters, solidifying who we are in Christ. When it comes to chapter 2:8-10, we see the end of the progression. Colossians 2:8-10 says:

> *Beware lest anyone cheat you through philosophy and empty deceit, according to the tradition of men, according to the basic principles of the world, and not according to Christ. For in Him dwells all the fullness of the Godhead bodily; and you are complete in Him, who is the head of all principality and power.*

Verses 9 and 10 say:

> *For in Him dwells all the **play-ro-mah** of the Godhead bodily; and you are **play-ro-o** in Him....*

This passage encourages us to expect to see the **fullness** of God manifested through our lives as we join in teamwork with others in the church. Hoping for anything less means we have been cheated in our expectation. When **play-ro-o** appears as a perfect participle passive, it emphasizes action taken in the past, which is still continually working on the subject (all believers) to complete their original goal. Are we there? Is going there even a goal? How much do we believe God has really done for us? *The Amplified Bible* does a good job of trying to bring this concept home. Colossians 2:9-10 in the Amplified says:

> *For in Him the whole **fullness** of Deity (the Godhead), continues to dwell in bodily form—giving complete*

expression of the divine nature. And you are in Him, made
full *and have come to **fullness** of life—in Christ you too are*
filled *with the Godhead: Father, Son and Holy Spirit, and*
*reach **full** spiritual stature. And He is the Head of all rule*
and authority of every angelic principality and power.

Why do we as church members expect our leaders to possess and walk in all the marks, while we follow? Christianity has never been a spectator sport. The Bible clearly and specifically proclaims in Colossians 2:10, "And you are **play-ro-o** in Him...." **Play-ro-o** is the verb. It speaks of action. Can we dare believe God wants to manifest action through us of the nature and character of the Father, and of the Son, and of the Spirit? Have our traditions, according to Colossians 2:8, seriously sold us short in what kind of action we need to believe God wants to perform through us individually and corporately? The answer to that is an unqualified, "Absolutely." Why do we not have the confidence to believe what the Bible says? Is it because we have never walked through the Spirit's doorway of ultimate commitment like the early church?

John 1:14-16 says:

And the Word became flesh and dwelt among us, and we
beheld His glory the glory as of the only begotten of the
Father, full [play-race] *of grace and truth. John bore*
witness of Him and cried out, saying, This was He of whom
I said, "He who comes after me is preferred before me, for He
was before me." And of His fullness [play-ro-mah] *we have*
all received, and grace for grace.

The gospel of John adds to the witness of the declaration of Colossians, and it says we have received of the **fullness** of Christ. We now have two witnesses in scripture to the fact God's intent for us is to progressively move into God's **fullness**.

Fullness—Paul's View

The Thread and Theme of Ephesians

The pinnacle of the New Testament revelation concerning church comes from the book of Ephesians. If Paul's prayers reflect the

Father's heart, we can postulate about the importance of fullness in God's plan for every believer.

> *Therefore I also, after I heard of your faith in the Lord Jesus and your love for all the saints, do not cease to give thanks for you, making mention of you in my prayers; that the God of our Lord Jesus Christ, the Father of glory, may give to you the spirit of wisdom and revelation in the knowledge of Him, the eyes of your understanding being enlightened; that you may know what is the hope of His calling, what are the riches of the glory of His inheritance in the saints, and what is the exceeding greatness of His power toward us who believe, according to the working of His mighty power which He worked in Christ when He raised Him from the dead and seated Him at His right hand in the heavenly places, far above all principality and power and might and dominion, and every name that is named, not only in this age but also in that which is to come. And He put all things under His feet, and gave Him to be head over all things to the church, which is His body, the fullness of Him who fills all in all.*
>
> *Ephesians 1:15-23*

In verses 22 and 23, Paul defines the church as "...the fullness of Him...." This is an amazing statement, "...which is His body, the **play-ro-mah** of Him who **play-ro-o** fills all in all." Are we living up to God's definition of the church? The church must experience a season where we are doing all that Jesus did.

Ephesians 2:18-22 once again alludes to the **fullness** of God:

> *For through Him we both have access by one Spirit to the Father. Now, therefore, you are no longer strangers and foreigners, but fellow citizens with the saints and members of the household of God, having been built on the foundation of the apostles and prophets, Jesus Christ Himself being the chief cornerstone, in whom the whole building, being joined together, grows into a holy temple in the Lord, in whom you also are being built together for a habitation of God in the Spirit.*

Verse 22 says our purpose is "...being built together for a habitation of God in the Spirit." God's purpose for us as a body is to manifest His **fullness**. Ephesians 3 enumerates another prayer for the realization of what has been bought and paid for by Jesus. If we can comprehend it, then surely we can believe for it!

Ephesians 3:14-18 says:

> For this reason I bow my knees to the Father of our Lord Jesus Christ, from whom the whole family in heaven and earth is named, that He would grant you, according to the riches of His glory, to be strengthened with might through His Spirit in the inner man, that Christ may dwell in your hearts through faith; that you, being rooted and grounded in love, may be able to comprehend with all the saints what is the width and length and depth and height....

The progression leads us to seeing, understanding, and asking God to manifest the promise of verse 19:

> ...to know the love of Christ which passes knowledge; that you may be **play-ro-o** with all the **play-ro-mah** of God.

The statement of Ephesians 3:19 is absolutely awesome in Greek concerning the issue of **fullness**. It says, **"eis pan to' play-ro-mah tou theou"** which means that we may become a body wholly filled and flooded by God, every pore vibrating with the creative power of The Trinity: replacing missing body parts, turning spoken words into reality, and moving medical mountains. Embracing and understanding fullness is our path toward possessing the "signs and wonders" mark of Acts 2:22. It says, "Men of Israel, hear these words: Jesus of Nazareth, a Man attested by God to you by miracles, wonders, and signs which God did through Him in your midst, as you yourselves also know—" The same mark or attestation, is to be upon believers according to Mark's account of the great commission, "And these signs will follow those who believe: In my name they will cast out demons; they will speak with new tongues...they will lay hands on the sick and they will recover." Ephesians outlines the path to receiving this mark.

We are beginning to see a thread emerging throughout the book of Ephesians. Ephesians 4:9-13 tells us God's plan for manifesting **fullness**. We are told:

> *(Now this, "He ascended"—what does it mean but that He also first descended into the lower parts of the earth? He who descended is also the One who ascended far above all the heavens, that He might fill all things.) And He Himself gave some to be apostles, some prophets, some evangelists, and some pastors and teachers, for the equipping of the saints for the work of ministry, for the edifying of the body of Christ, till we all come to the unity of the faith and the knowledge of the Son of God, to a perfect man, to the measure of the stature of the **fullness** of Christ....*

The five-fold ministry has one purpose in God's plan and that is to grow the body until we can all begin to walk in "...the measure of the stature of the **play-ro-mah** of Christ."

Ephesians 5:18 says:

> *And do not be drunk with wine, in which is dissipation; but be **filled** with the Spirit....*

This passage exhorts us to demonstrate the **fullness** of God through faith-filled action. The same thread continues all the way through the book of Ephesians, ending in Ephesians 6:10-20 with the exhortation to "Put on the whole armor of God." The book of Ephesians is generally accepted as presenting the pinnacle revelation of the church in the New Testament. Ephesians has a single consistent thread of thought, **play-ro-mah**, running straight through, declaring God's intent for the church in the last days. Every chapter of Ephesians exhorts us to believe for **fullness**.

Fullness—John's View

There are a number of places throughout the gospels promising us the joy of being filled with each individual of the Trinity—thus confirming fullness. John 16:7-13 promises us the Spirit:

> *Nevertheless I tell you the truth. It is to your advantage that I go away; for if I do not go away, the Helper will not come*

to you; but if I depart, I will send Him to you. And when He has come, He will convict the world of sin, and of righteousness, and of judgment: of sin, because they do not believe in Me; of righteousness, because I go to My Father and you see Me no more; of judgment, because the ruler of this world is judged. I still have many things to say to you, but you cannot bear them now. However, when He, the Spirit of truth, has come He will guide you into all truth; for He will not speak on His own authority, but whatever He hears He will speak; and He will tell you things to come.

In John 14:22 and 23, Jesus makes it very clear that He and the Father will come and take up residence. John says:

Judas (not Iscariot) said to Him, "Lord, how is it that You will manifest Yourself to us, and not to the world?" Jesus answered and said to him, "If anyone loves Me, he will keep My word; and My Father will love him, and We will come to him and make Our home with him."

Jesus promised **fullness**.

In Revelation 3:14-20, we are invited to enter an open door:

And to the angel of the church of the Laodiceans write, "These things says the Amen, the Faithful and True Witness, the Beginning of the creation of God: I know your works, that you are neither cold nor hot. I could wish you were cold or hot. So then, because you are lukewarm, and neither cold nor hot, I will spew you out of My mouth. Because you say, 'I am rich, have become wealthy, and have need of nothing'—and do not know that you are wretched, miserable, poor, blind, and naked — I counsel you to buy from Me gold refined in the fire, that you may be rich; and white garments, that you may be clothed, that the shame of your nakedness may not be revealed; and anoint your eyes with eye salve, that you may see. As many as I love, I rebuke and chasten. Therefore be zealous and repent. Behold, I stand at the door and knock. If anyone hears My voice and opens the door, I will come in to him and dine with him, and he with Me."

Jesus counseled the Laodicean church to buy from Him, gold refined in the fire; "...to buy from Jesus gold refined in the fire..." is to make the same commitment to our Father that Jesus made to His Father. "God, here is my life, spend it any way You want." We must make a radical commitment. That commitment is a doorway in the Spirit. When we walk through it, we buy the true gold refined in the fire.

Since we do not have that commitment in much of the church today, how do we develop it? Jesus by example taught us that once we commit to martyrdom and give God our life, no one can take that life until we have finished our race. Jesus gave such a stirring message in His own hometown in Luke 4:18-30 that the response was overwhelming. Verses 28-30 say:

> *Then all those in the synagogue, when they heard these things, were filled with wrath, And rose up and thrust Him out of the city; and they led Him to the brow of the hill on which their city was built, that they might throw Him down over the cliff. Then passing through the midst of them, He went His way.*

Jesus made the commitment to sow his life and no one could end it until He reached personal **fullness**. In John 19:10 and 11, Pilate said to Jesus, "Do You not know that I have power to crucify You, and power to release You? Jesus answered, 'You could have no power at all against Me unless it had been given you from above.'"

The apostle Paul writing from a Roman jail, waiting for the verdict of the Imperial Court, sounds just like Jesus:

> *For to me, to live is Christ, and to die is gain. But if I live on in the flesh, this will mean fruit from my labor; yet what I shall choose I cannot tell. For I am hard pressed between the two, having a desire to depart and be with Christ, which is far better. Nevertheless to remain in the flesh is more needful for you. And being confident of this, I know that I shall remain and continue with you all for your progress and joy of faith, That your rejoicing for me may be more abundant in Jesus Christ by my coming to you again.*

> *Philippians 1:21-26*

In Paul's mind, his death was not in the hands of the ultimate Roman Court, but an issue of whether or not he had completed all heavenly assignments. Paul made his commitment to martyrdom in Acts 21:13b, "For I am ready not only to be bound, but also to die at Jerusalem for the name of the Lord Jesus." Paul knew he would not die in Jerusalem, although a dramatic attempt was made. God had revealed His plan for Paul to witness in Rome. In Paul's understanding, nothing could take his life until every assignment was fulfilled. He chose to "lay his life down" and no one could take it from him before attaining ministerial fullness.

When we volunteer all we have, God promises protection until we reach individual **fullness**. When we choose to "lose our life" is when we really find it. Walking through the spiritual door of offering our life to God to lay down as He pleases is the only way to guarantee divine protection until we finish the race. Whatever we hold back from God is vulnerable to the enemy. Whatever is not entrusted to God may be stolen by Satan. God chooses when and how to bring us home. If He does so in high school or college, it is for His purpose, which usually only eternity can count. I lost a close cousin my same age the week we graduated from high school. My aunt, who lost her son, said to me at the funeral home as we were viewing the body, "Now you will have to do the work of two!" God chose that event to mark my life. No one else would have chosen such an event for that purpose (certainly not my cousin's parents), but God reserves the right to spend us as He wills!

God, here's my life...spend it

Any way You want to,

May my commitment

Rest firmly in You.

To follow the Savior

Is my heart's desire,

Humbly walking where He walked

Gold proved in the fire.

CHAPTER 10

The Double Anointing

Walking in the full measure of Christ for many may mean a theological transformation. Those of us who tend to judge the events of life by John 10:10 may want to expand our theological reservoir to accommodate an additional flow of understanding.

> The thief does not come except to steal, and to kill, and to destroy. I have come that they may have life, and that they may have it more abundantly.

Many have been encouraged to look at every adversity through the eyes of John 10:10. Did God intend this passage to be such a yardstick? If we are pulling it out of context then we may at times unknowingly be misapplying it. The context of John 10:10 speaks to the issue of pharisaism and how it distorts and blinds people to discerning the real. When we talk about preparing for the double anointing, we are really saying we need to be vessels trained to encounter every purpose, available to respond according to the pattern of scripture. If we viewed the New Testament through John 10:10, as our yardstick of judging what comes from God and what comes from the enemy, we could be blinded to a whole dimension of divine preparation outlined in the context of John 9.

John 9:39 says:

> And Jesus said, "For judgment I have come into this world, that those who do not see may see, and that those who see may be made blind."

A good example of what is meant by this is prophesied by Isaiah chapter 61. Isaiah saw a progressive ministry of Jesus, but apparently had no idea that it would be divided in two parts. The first part involved an earthly three and a half year ministry, and the second was reserved for the season after the ascension when Jesus was seated at the right hand of God. Isaiah saw one continuous stream. Isaiah 61:1-2 says:

> *The Spirit of the LORD God is upon Me, Because the LORD has anointed Me To preach good tidings to the poor; He has sent Me to heal the brokenhearted, To proclaim liberty to the captives, And the opening of the prison to those who are bound; To proclaim the acceptable year of the LORD, And the day of vengeance of our God;*

He saw blessing and deliverance along with **judgment** and captivity. What Isaiah saw together, God separated for emphasis. Isaiah saw two streams: co-existent but different. Isaiah 61:1-2 end with "...vengeance of our God...." Isaiah saw jubilee and judgment flowing together. Jesus was limited to birthing salvation during His earthly ministry, but entered the judgment stream after His ascension and seating at the right hand of the Father.

In Matthew 10:5-8 we find:

> *These twelve Jesus sent out and commanded them, saying: "Do not go into the way of the Gentiles, and do not enter a city of the Samaritans. But go rather to the lost sheep of the house of Israel. And as you go, preach, saying, 'The kingdom of heaven is at hand' Heal the sick, cleanse the lepers, raise the dead, cast out demons. Freely you have received, freely give."*

Here we see Jesus anointing the Twelve and sending them out to accomplish a specific purpose.

In Revelation 2:5, speaking both correction and warning to the church at Ephesus, Jesus said:

> *Remember therefore from where you have fallen; repent and do the first works, or else I will come to you quickly and remove your lampstand from its place—unless you repent.*

In Matthew 10, Jesus lights the lampstand of anointing and sends people forth in the power of the Spirit. In Revelation 2, speaking to the church at Ephesus, Jesus said, "If you don't repent, I'll remove your lampstand." Isaiah saw these two streams merged as one ministry. In the gospels, Jesus helps the sick recover, but in Revelation 2:22 He says if you do not repent, **"I will *throw you into a sickbed.*"** In the gospels, Jesus continually heals the sick and in Revelation 2 He says, "If you don't repent I'll make you sick." The biggest problem in teaching this comes from the assumptions of those seeking healing but not receiving it. The accuser of the brethren is quick to whisper, "The sin in your life is blocking your healing," when a third option is far more likely. If the problem were sin, James 5 covers it by promising if we call the elders, they will pray the "prayer of faith" which heals the sick and if there is any sin, it will be forgiven.

The third option in waiting for healing is the issue of fullness which when in operation spiritually identifies us with a generation in Egypt just before the great exodus. Psalm 105:25 reveals God's hand in the adversity of believers leading to the great judgments which produce liberty for the captives once fullness is complete by the Egyptians. It appears seasons of adversity endured by God's people pay the price for covenant justice setting the stage for great deliverance. Romans 8:28-39 reveals just such a season as it explains the intercession of Psalm 44:10-22. Paying the price of fullness frees us from looking for non-existent or unresolved sin and preserves our relationship with the Lord enabling fruitfulness instead of bitterness. For a more comprehensive treatment of this issue as it relates to healing, see the CD series "The Path, Price & Power of the Plumbline."

If we have been taught God does not do what Revelation 2:22 says, we have two choices. We can either 1) take a pen knife and cut out Revelation 2, and any other chapter which contradicts our theology (and they seem numerous), or 2) realize our lack of biblical understanding, and pray for more water to expand the "reservoir."

Luke 7:11-15 says:

> *Now it happened, the day after, that He went into a city called Nain; and many of His disciples went with Him, and*

a large crowd. And when He came near the gate of the city, behold, a dead man was being carried out, the only son of his mother; and she was a widow. And a large crowd from the city was with her. When the Lord saw her, He had compassion on her and said to her, "Do not weep." Then He came and touched the open coffin, and those who carried him stood still. And He said, "Young man, I say to you, arise." And he who was dead sat up and began to speak. And He presented him to his mother.

In the gospels, Jesus raises the dead. But in Acts 5 and Revelation chapter 2, if they refuse to repent, He makes them dead. In the gospels, Jesus stills the storm and brings peace, but in Revelation 2:22 He says: "...if you don't repent, I shall send great tribulation." I fully support teaching faith to elevate the level of victory within the church, but I vehemently oppose denying scripture and misleading people, telling them "God does not ever send adversity." God seems to have expounded enough principles which conflict to prohibit ministry-by-formula. Each situation must be discerned, and appropriate spirit-led action initiated.

God has engineered theology and our lives in such a way as to necessitate ministry from personal relationship. Once we embrace a formula and consistently regurgitate it, we sound like a clanging cymbal or tinkling bell (1 Corinthians 13:1)—it just does not fit every circumstance. A major contribution to the lack of "fear of the Lord" in the church lies at the feet of ministers who have consistently denied "Jesus the Judge" in the misdirected attempt to build a ministry on half the Word. What happened when Jesus ascended and was seated at the right hand of God? God rewarded His obedience by adding **"Judge of all the earth"** to His ministry! We must recognize as we approach the end of the age that **fullness** of God and iniquity will be growing progressively in two distinct and diametrically opposite camps. We must develop faith to participate in dispensing the judgments of God. We must prepare the church for dramatic spiritual confrontations. The end-time picture is Revelation 22:11:

He who is unjust, let him be unjust still; he who is filthy, let him be filthy still; he who is righteous, let him be righteous still; he who is holy, let him be holy still.

The end-times are marked by confrontations between individuals filled with their respective lords. Acts 5:1-5 reveals two people filled with two entirely different spirits facing off with each other:

> *But a certain man named Ananias, with Sapphira his wife, sold a possession. And he kept back part of the proceeds, his wife also being aware of it, and brought a certain part and laid it at the apostles' feet. But Peter said, "Ananias, why has Satan* **play-ro-o** *your heart to lie to the Holy Spirit and keep back part of the price of the land for yourself? While it remained, was it not your own? And after it was sold, was it not in your own control? Why have you conceived this thing in your heart? You have not lied to men but to God." Then Ananias, hearing these words, fell down and breathed his last. So great fear came upon all those who heard these things.*

How much "fear of the Lord" resides in the church? Have decades of seeker-sensitivity Christianity stolen the "fear of the Lord?" It is only when the **fullness** of God begins to manifest in the church through judgment that the "fear of the Lord" is restored. Will God restore the "fear of the Lord?" Is a restoration needed in today's church? Where is the fear by which we persuade men? Does God demand a price for birthing the "fear of the Lord?"

Acts 13 is another example of two individuals brought to confrontation by being filled with their respective masters. Acts 13:6-12 says:

> *Now when they had gone through the island of Paphos, they found a certain sorcerer, a false prophet, a Jew whose name was Bar-Jesus, who was with the proconsul, Sergius Paulus, an intelligent man. This man called for Barnabas and Saul and sought to hear the word of God. But Elymas the sorcerer (for so his name is translated) withstood them, seeking to turn the proconsul away from the faith. Then Saul, who also is called Paul,* **play-tho filled** *with the Holy Spirit, looked intently at him and said, "O full* [play-race] *(one filled) of all deceit and all fraud, you son of the devil, you enemy of all righteousness, will you not cease perverting the straight*

ways of the Lord? And now, indeed, the hand of the Lord is upon you, and you shall be blind, not seeing the sun for a time" And immediately a dark mist fell on him, and he went around seeking someone to lead him by the hand. Then the proconsul believed, when he saw what had been done, being astonished at the teaching [did-akh-ay] (doctrine) *of the Lord.*

We have an account of the confrontation between two individuals both full of their respective lords. The issue is not if we will face the same thing but **when**. We can expect it! If we were to face a similar encounter, are we prepared? Do we have God's marks? What saith our spirit at the thought of facing an Elymas? If we have peace, we are probably prepared. If we think, "Jesus is coming to rapture me out of here—I will not encounter an Elymas," then we have a false peace that could evaporate in a heartbeat. Now is the time to prepare—be diligent! God has an answer for people who are full of the devil, and the answer is His fully marked men and women manifested to bring judgment, setting free all who are bound. The blindness that came on Elymas was not from the devil. It was from God. Speaking judgment into existence was necessary in order for Paul to gain access to the appointed region and win the political leader. How much territory continues in captivity because we are without God's full preparation or because we have been taught God does not judge? How many **ethnos** remain under the influence of self-seeking, personal kingdom builders masquerading as ministers? Many of our teachers have not led us to embrace the **did-akh-ay** (doctrine) of the Lord which includes judgment. We as a church desperately need the **fullness** of God manifested in our lives. The early church moved in it. Will it not also be part of an end-time restoration? Training begins with "**The Sure Mercies of David.**"

It must come in multiplied measure. Are we preparing?

Let us set our sights on being fully marked of God. We must move out of our comfortable, fenced-in pasture. We should feed on the green grass of who we are in Christ. Let the Word become the firm foundation of our radical obedience.

Romans 8:22-30 says:

For we know that the whole creation groans and labors with birth pangs together until now. And not only they, but we also who have the first-fruits of the Spirit, even we ourselves groan within ourselves, eagerly waiting for the adoption, the redemption of our body. For we were saved in this hope, but hope that is seen is not hope; for why does one still hope for what he sees? But if we hope for what we do not see, then we eagerly wait for it with perseverance. Likewise the Spirit also helps in our weaknesses. For we do not know what we should pray for as we ought, but the Spirit Himself makes intercession for us with groanings which cannot be uttered.

Now He who searches the hearts knows what the mind of the Spirit is, because He makes intercession for the saints according to the will of God. And we know that all things work together for good to those who love God, to those who are the called according to His purpose. For those whom He foreknew—of whom He was aware and loved beforehand—He also destined from the beginning (foreordaining them) to be molded into the image of His Son [and share inwardly His likeness], that He might become the first-born among many brethren (the Amplified Bible). Moreover whom He predestined, these He also called; whom He called, these He also justified; and whom He justified, these He also glorified.

New Testament Thinking

If we choose to set our sights on the reality of Romans 8:29, "being conformed to His image," God answers our longing by moving in our families for the purpose of finishing a preparational work.

Hebrews 12:18-24 presents the same thread as Romans 8:

For you have not come to the mountain that may be touched and that burned with fire, and to blackness and darkness and tempest, and the sound of a trumpet and the voice of words, so that those who heard it begged that the word should not be spoken to them anymore. (For they could not endure what was commanded: "And if so much as a beast touches the mountain, it shall be stoned or thrust through with an arrow." And so terrifying was the sight that Moses said, "I am exceedingly afraid and trembling.") But you have come to Mount Zion and to the city of the living God, the heavenly Jerusalem, to an innumerable company of angels, to the general assembly and church of the firstborn who are registered in heaven, to God the Judge of all, to the spirits of just men made perfect, to Jesus the Mediator of the new covenant, and to the blood of sprinkling that speaks better things than that of Abel.

The writer of Hebrews helps us understand a major transition in the Spirit from the Old Covenant to the New. Unlike the law of the Old, we have not come to a truth that is only seen and cannot be fully embraced. We have come to a reality, Mount Zion. We have been members of the "...church of the firstborn..." and the only way we attain entrance is to be born into it. Every baby who is born moves toward the reality of adulthood. Every person truly born into the church starts growing up into the likeness of Jesus. There is only one path to spiritual adulthood—the life of Jesus. If we are going to follow the pattern of Jesus, and Hebrews clearly tells us we must, then chapter 10, verses 1-7 becomes foundational as we view Jesus as the prototype of a family through which God intends to accomplish His purposes. Hebrews 10:7 demonstrates the fiber of this family.

Then I said, "Behold, I have come—In the volume of the book it is written of Me—To do Your will, O God."

The unique thing about the Jesus of Hebrews 10:7 is He was wholly given over to accomplish the will of His Father. This attitude ruled His life and was His heart's motivation. Most of us would admit we are really not quite there yet. That brings us to the question of how do we go from where we are now to the place where the motivation which ruled the life of Jesus begins to dominate and govern our lives? One answer may be in Hebrews 10:8-22, continuing the progression, where we are challenged to transition from the Old Testament representative-ministry mentality to being designated kings and priests with a personal invitation to the Throne Room. We can assume our church leadership will do our warfare for us, or we can rise to the challenge. You were called to be a priest and a king. Do not leave it to your pastor! As long as the church continues to fill convention centers for healing ministries, we prove we are still entrenched in Old Testament patterns. The Old Testament must now be interpreted in the light of the New if we want the promised results.

> *Previously saying, "Sacrifice and offering, burnt offerings, and offerings for sin You did not desire, nor had pleasure in them" (which are offered according to the law), then He said, "Behold, I have come to do Your will, O God," He takes away the first that He may establish the second.*

> *Hebrews 10:8-9*

If God really took the first covenant away, why do we have such difficulty embracing the changes? Pentecostal pioneers had a favorite saying, "The New Testament is in the Old Covenant concealed, while the Old Testament is in the New Testament revealed." In many ways, the church seems to manifest a mentality from using the reverse of this principle. Old Testament thinking really hinders individual acceptance of spiritual responsibility and growth toward maturity. In the Old Testament, the priests were responsible for ministry, while in the New, we are all priests.

We have spent a lifetime developing a priestly ministry mentality. In that mindset, we are always bringing salvation to the individual. Extending mercy to everyone is our M.O. (Method of Operation). Extending mercy is great unless the individual is a Balaam, Absalom or Jezebel. God did not extend mercy to these destroyers of Israel but we do. Why are we so reluctant to represent Jesus the Judge? (see *The Sure Mercies of David*, "Jesus & Justice" and "A Heart for War" CD series).

The Father's fullness in our lives

Works healing and deliverance,

But the time will one day come

When fullness stands a judgment stance.

If we adhere to raptured-out

We may be caught most unaware,

Perhaps a target, easy prey

Left behind and unprepared.

CHAPTER 11

Two Preparational Veils

We must live, spiritually speaking, in the holy of holies, and the only way to get there is to go through the veil. Jesus paved the way and left a pattern to follow. Whether we are going to visit or to live there, the pathway is still the same. Doing what Jesus did results from choosing to pay the price of passing through the veils. Passing through the first two becomes the path and pattern for the third, resulting in the final marks.

The first veil is in 2 Corinthians 3:7-15:

> But if the ministry of death, written and engraved on stones, was glorious, so that the children of Israel could not look steadily at the face of Moses because of the glory of his countenance, which glory was passing away, how will the ministry of the Spirit not be more glorious? For if the ministry of condemnation had glory, the ministry of righteousness exceeds much more in glory. For even what was made glorious had no glory in this respect, because of the glory that excels. For if what is passing away was glorious, what remains is much more glorious. Therefore, since we have such hope, we use great boldness of speech—unlike Moses, who put a veil over his face so that the children of Israel could not look steadily at the end of what was passing away. But their minds were hardened. For until this day the same veil remains unlifted in the reading of the Old Testament, because the veil is taken away in

> *Christ. But even to this day, when Moses is read, a veil lies on their heart.*

What is the first veil in scripture we have to walk through? It is not complex. Most of us have already come through it. It is a revelation of the fact that we need a Savior. It is a revelation of our sin and willingness to do what God prescribed when we realize we have been snared. The first veil may seem obvious, but it reveals the pattern for passing through all three. The Greek word translated "veil" is **kal-oo-mah** and it means to cover, encircle, or place around as an impediment to understanding.

This first veil is over the heart and concerns the issue of blindness to sin, the need for salvation and Jesus as Savior. The process for moving through each of the three veils is emphasized in the picture of the first as verses 16-18 demonstrate:

> *Nevertheless when one turns to the Lord, the veil is taken away. Now the Lord is the Spirit; and where the Spirit of the Lord is, there is liberty. But we all, with unveiled face, beholding as in a mirror the glory of the Lord, are being transformed into the same image from glory to glory, just as by the Spirit of the Lord.*

The key concept in verse 16 is the Greek word **epi-stref-o**, translated **"turns."**

> *Nevertheless when one turns to the Lord, the veil is taken away.*

Epi-stref-o means to literally do a sharp action in the form of a military about-face. It is pointed, decisive and resolute! This same word appears in Acts 3:19 promising us great blessing when we walk in repentance:

> *Repent therefore and be **converted** [epi-stref-o-te], that your sins may be blotted out, so that times of refreshing may come from the presence of the Lord....*

This very same concept appears in Mark 4 in the parable of the sower and becomes, according to Jesus, the foundation for understanding all the parables of the New Testament. Jesus said in Mark 4:11-12:

And He said to them, "To you it has been given to know the mystery of the kingdom of God; but to those who are outside, all things come in parables, so that 'Seeing they may see and not perceive, And hearing they may hear and not understand; Lest they should turn [epi-stref-o], And their sins be forgiven them"

The Power of Turning

In the parable of the sower, Jesus teaches we face a variety of obstacles to fruitfulness typified by four different kinds of soil. Wayside soil means the seed never gets a chance to germinate because the ground is so hard the birds can pick up the seed right after it is sown. In wayside soil, preparation has been inadequate for planting usually by refusing the plowing process. In the stony ground there is germination, but the stones are so hard, root can never develop and it therefore withers prematurely. In the third kind of soil, the seed germinates and develops roots, but is then overtaken by thorns. The whole point of the parable is how to overcome unproductive attitudes and develop good soil. The willingness of believers to turn (**epi-stref-o**) when the Lord lifts a veil and we see things from an eternal perspective is the key to attaining all the marks. Why do people turn to God? Because suddenly they begin to accept the view God presents. They begin to see themselves as they really are.

In Mark 4:21-25, Jesus said:

And He said to them, "Is a lamp brought to be put under a basket or under a bed? Is it not to be set on a lampstand? For there is nothing hidden which will not be revealed, nor has anything been kept secret but that it should come to light. If anyone has ears to hear, let him hear." And He said to them, "Take heed what you hear. With the same measure you use, it will be measured to you; and to you who hear, more will be given. For whoever has, to him more will be given; but whoever does not have, even what he has will be taken away from him."

This parable promises we can reach the pinnacle of our gifting and calling if we develop but one attribute—a readiness to execute an about-face (**epi-stref-o**). If we develop that attitude, more will be given. But whoever does not have a willingness to repent (**epi-stref-o**) hardens his heart and will eventually lose all he has!

As we approach the end of the age, the issue of having a repentant heart becomes more and more the determining factor in how far we go with God.

The same principle guarantees **fullness** when unveiled. If we turn, the reward is a progression toward all God has. If we refuse, the reward is a progression toward the mark of an outlaw spirit. The same process that takes us to **fullness** of God will take people who refuse to deal with unrighteous areas of their lives to **fullness** of the enemy. **Fullness** in the last days also governs the religious system. How does the process work? God says it is time to go from glory to glory. He comes and lifts the lid on specific areas of life. We begin to see things that are in us which we haven't seen before. Then we exercise a choice to either accept the divine assessment and deal with it or walk away from the demanded changes. If we choose to turn from personal weakness and failure, we are guaranteed space on the pathway to fulfilling God's purposes.

When we refuse correction, what usually happens is an offense develops and we run from the place God has chosen to deal with us—resulting in strengthening the sin and a progression toward developing a demonic stronghold. The same principle of spiritual growth to maturity governs both kingdoms of light and darkness. The growth pattern is "...first the blade, then the ear, then the full corn in the ear." The Pharisees did not become full-blown Pharisees overnight. They **grew** into that blinded, hardened condition. And we grow progressively, just as they did, based on our choices. A blinded, hardened condition results by refusing to deal with areas of our flesh when God brings them to the surface. God honors repentance by a progressive impartation of divine redemption and restoration. The same process, depending on how we respond, will take us into one of two streams in the last days. There are only two. We are either going to be full of God, or full of another spirit. The days of half-hearted church participation are progressively coming to an end! Who do we think sheds the blood that fills the cup in the book of Revelation? The world is not that interested. It is the demonized followers of a counterfeit religion. Of which group will we be a part? It all depends on what we do when unveiled! The growth pattern, "...first the blade, then the ear, then the full corn in the ear" describes this progression.

Generally, in scripture, individual failure is not the ultimate limiting factor in fulfilling our eternal call. Personal failure did not disqualify Moses, David or Paul. They all had one thing in common—a heart that would readily **epi-stref-o**. God met Moses to kill him en route to Egypt because he had not been obedient in circumcising his sons because of Zipporah. Moses quickly did an "about-face!" God met David through the voice of Nathan the prophet, and David quickly turned after being confronted with the Bathsheba and Uriah incident. God met Saul of Tarsus on the road to Damacus and Saul, being blinded, did not know which way to turn (God must enjoy comic relief). The issue has never been the nature or magnitude of our personal failures, but rather our willingness to change when God lifts the veil and reveals our condition.

2 Corinthians 3:16-18 says:

> *Nevertheless when one turns* [epi-stref-o's] *to the Lord, the veil is taken away. Now the Lord is the Spirit; and where the Spirit of the Lord is, there is liberty. But we all, with unveiled face, beholding as in a mirror the glory of the Lord, are being transformed into the same image from glory to glory, just as by the Spirit of the Lord.*

The pattern of verse 18 clearly outlines our growth toward the **fullness** of God. For us to grow, God has to come and unveil us so we see in His mirror our true condition. Only then can we be transformed. Only then can we change. Every church that resists true prophetic words spiritually spits in God's face. God sends His servants with a word that unveils personal or corporate activities, demanding acknowledgment. When confronted, most churches verbally stone the messenger, assassinate his character and refuse to turn. They justify their actions by finding and criticizing a personal flaw in the messenger. God uses flawed messengers to test the humility and obedience of the church. When churches "spit in a true prophet's face," that prophet has an option of praying a priestly prayer, "Father, forgive them for they know not what they do" or praying kingly, "But You, O God, shall bring them down to the pit of destruction; Bloodthirsty and deceitful men shall not live out half their days; But I will trust in You."

How many times have we quoted, "from glory to glory" not having a clue what we were declaring? In all the times we quoted this passage as believers, we probably never guessed the extent of divine intervention for which we were ultimately demanding! Every time we quoted "from glory to glory," we asked God to unveil us at His discretion—at the depth of His choice with flawed messengers who we could hardly recognize. We either humble ourselves and receive or arrogantly reject, criticize and assassinate.

We must cry "God, give us eyes to see!" Only then can we **epi-stref-o**.

Pattern for Turning

God's pattern for going through each of the three veils is always the same. He first comes to unveil us and, if we humble ourselves to receive, we suddenly see our nakedness. We are now forced to make a personal choice. This process raises an issue which only has two options. The first option is preferred because of its eternal fruit. In option one, we see, acknowledge and turn, allowing the Lord to permanently remove the veil. In option two, we deny the obvious and run from the truth, preserving the facade and hiding the pain. This forfeits God's blessing through kingdom advancement and usually results in camping under the cover of plasticized Christianity in a do-anything-but-deal-with-the-heart church, having a "form of godliness" but denying the cross. Not everyone who comes to church wants their hearts dealt with! Have you noticed? Social clubs abound masquerading as churches. One way you can usually tell you are in a social club is all the messages conform to "Franchise Standards." "We just want a family church—so whatever you do, do not open the barn door and by all means, do not shovel out the manure." Prophets know the best harvests are produced when all the fertilizer has been removed from the barn and spread on the field.

In Luke 12:1-2, we see the depth of Jesus' commitment to unveil us so we can have the opportunity of turning. Luke 12:1-2 says:

> *In the meantime, when an innumerable multitude of people had gathered together, so that they trampled one another, He began to say to His disciples first of all, "Beware of the leaven of the Pharisees, which is hypocrisy. For there is nothing covered that will not be revealed, nor hidden that will not be known."*

We serve a God who is absolutely committed, above everything else, to unveiling us year by year so we can step into His **fullness**. Wherever we have hypocrisy as a cancer eating away at the body, Jesus is committed to come and unveil that which is hindering us from fulfilling His perfect will. When God comes in a new move of the Spirit, there is always an unveiling that accompanies the move. The Toronto Blessing was a perfect historical example of God's unveiling by a **kairos** move of the Spirit. The spiritual intellectuals and those possessed by religious spirits kept asking, "Why would God ever send a laughing revival?" God gave the answer to prophets, but those of us walking in our "head" instead of our "heart" could not receive. Receiving the "laughing revival" was usually very humiliating to the flesh, a great study for abnormal spiritual psychology. Perhaps this "humiliation" was the real objection of intellectual arrogance, resulting in rejection. Through the Toronto Blessing, God encouraged the church to continue believing for the progression of Psalm 2. God demands the right to prepare His church to harvest cities and nations! God unveiled massive pharisaism by moving on people to laugh.

In Isaiah 6, when the prophet encountered the Lord, there was a tremendous unveiling of his heart. Isaiah 6:1-8 says:

> *In the year that King Uzziah died, I saw the LORD sitting on a throne, high and lifted up, and the train of His robe filled the temple. Above it stood seraphim; each one had six wings: with two he covered his face, with two he covered his feet, and with two he flew. And one cried to another and said: "Holy, holy holy is the LORD of hosts; The whole earth is full of His glory!" And the posts of the door were shaken*

*by the voice of him who cried out, and the house was filled
with smoke. Then I said: "Woe is me, for I am undone!
Because I am a man of unclean lips, And I dwell in the midst
of a people of unclean lips; For my eyes have seen the King,
The LORD of hosts." Then one of the seraphim flew to me,
having in his hand a live coal which he had taken with the
tongs from the altar. And he touched my mouth with it, and
said: "Behold, this has touched your lips; Your iniquity is
taken away, And your sin purged." Also I heard the voice of
the LORD, saying: "Whom shall I send, And who will go for
Us?"*

When Isaiah saw the Lord, the depth of unveiling was revealed
by his words. Isaiah's words are the response of a heart unveiled.

*Woe is me, for I am undone! Because I am a man of unclean
lips, And I dwell in the midst of a people of unclean lips; For
my eyes have seen the King, The LORD of hosts.*

When God comes, in whatever form, by direct visitation as He
did to Moses or in a move of the Spirit whether familiar or
unfamiliar, hearts are always revealed. The choice always involves
an **epi-stref-o**, an about-face. When we do our part and turn, we
secure deliverance and removal of the veil.

The Second Veil

The second major veil stresses the importance of adherence to
Jesus' final command before the Ascension. Many choose to neglect,
disregard or disdain divine empowering for ministry. In the book of
Acts, there are five places where people receive the Holy Spirit, and
all five indicate the sign of a supernatural prayer language enabling
the individuals to pray God's perfect will beyond the hindrance of
their own understanding. This empowering is essential to achieve
personal and corporate **fullness**. It has been steadfastly resisted in
every generation. In three of the five places in Acts where people
received the Holy Spirit, we are told they spoke in tongues, while
tongues are implied in the other two. Yet we still have many leaders
of the church fighting the very thing that would propel their

congregations forward. They have yet to walk through this veil. Acts 2:7 and 12 say:

> *Then they were all amazed and marveled, saying to one another, "Look, are not all these who speak Galileans?...."*
> *So they were all amazed and perplexed, saying to one another, "Whatever could this mean?"*

For years, some evangelical scholars have been telling us that those speaking in tongues were ecstatic, out of their mind. The word used for amazed is **ex-is-tan-to** which means "to astound, amaze, astonish, to wonder, or to put out of one's wits." The twisting of this passage is what truly amazes me. The very fact that anyone would read verses 7 and 12 and attempt to use that Greek word to characterize the people **speaking in tongues** shows the depth of the veil that is on their mindset over the issue of praying in tongues. It is very clear that verses 7 and 12 describe the people who are watching—not the ones who are speaking in other tongues. When a religious spirit comes to incarcerate and keep someone from the power of God, hindering their calling, the veil gets very thick. The reason why the enemy works so hard at veiling the church concerning the power of the Holy Spirit, and the value of the supernatural prayer language which goes with it, can be seen in Acts 2:33-35. It says:

> *Therefore being exalted to the right hand of God, and having received from the Father the promise of the Holy Spirit, He poured out this which you now see and hear. For David did not ascend into the heavens, but he says himself: "The LORD said to my Lord, 'Sit at My right hand, Till I make Your enemies Your footstool.'"*

The Holy Spirit and the prayer language of tongues form the beginning of the fulfillment of Jesus seated at the right hand of God making His enemies His footstool. Seven times in the New Testament we are given that statement. Seeing His enemies made our footstool is such an eternal commitment that God has spoken it to us seven times—the number of completion. When God says something seven times, we know He is either really committed or we are so dense that we need to hear it over and over! Is it any wonder the catalyst of bringing this victory seems to be veiled in every possible way?

1 Corinthians 14:7-9 shows us what God thinks of those who stand outside His empowering provision for fulfilling their ministry. He says in verses 7-16:

> *Even things without life, whether flute or harp, when they make a sound, unless they make a distinction in the sounds, how will it be known what is piped or played? For if the trumpet makes an uncertain sound, who will prepare himself for battle? So likewise you, unless you utter by the tongue words easy to understand, how will it be known what is spoken? For you will be speaking into the air. There are, it may be, so many kinds of languages in the world, and none of them is without significance. Therefore, if I do not know the meaning of the language, I shall be a foreigner to him who speaks, and he who speaks will be a foreigner to me. Even so you since you are zealous for spiritual gifts, let it be for the edification of the church that you seek to excel. Therefore let him who speaks in a tongue pray that he may interpret. For if I pray in a tongue, my spirit prays, but my understanding is unfruitful. What is the result then? I will pray with the spirit, and I will also pray with the understanding. I will sing with the spirit and I will sing with the understanding. Otherwise, if you bless with the spirit, how will he who occupies the place of the **uninformed** say "Amen" at your giving of thanks, since he does not understand what you say?*

Verse 16 reveals a glimpse of God's mindset when it uses a unique Greek word translated "uninformed." If we bless with the spirit, how will he who occupies the place of the "...uninformed agree or say 'Amen' at our giving of thanks...?" The Greek word translated "uninformed" is **id-ee-o-tace**. It is interesting to observe the Holy Spirit speaking through the apostle Paul, describing people in the church who are still veiled over the issue of the Holy Spirit as occupying the place of the **id-ee-o-tace**. It is one thing to suffer the humiliation of being assigned to the old-fashioned "dunce corner," but quite another to choose it and then be proud of it.

Why would anyone choose to be uninformed? In the interest of equity, **id-ee-o-tace** had a significantly different meaning two thousand years ago. It meant to be common as opposed to being a man of power and learning—what a statement! God's pathway to being a person of power and learning is to go through the veil which constitutes accepting and receiving the baptism of the Spirit. What have we substituted for power today? We have substituted education and getting our PhD's in theology. Becoming a Dr. does not guarantee freedom from occupying the place of an **id-ee-o-tace**. God's definition of a man of power and learning is one who walks through this second veil and moves into the fullness of the Holy Spirit. Verse 16 is not the only place the Holy Spirit called believers **id-ee-o-tace**. Verses 23 through 25 complete His thoughts on the issue.

> *Therefore if the whole church comes together in one place, and all speak with tongues, and there come in those who are **uninformed** or unbelievers, will they not say that you are out of your mind? But if all prophesy, and an unbeliever or an **uninformed** person comes in, he is convinced by all, he is judged by all. And thus the secrets of his heart are revealed; and so, falling down on his face, he will worship God and report that God is truly among you.*

Is God truly among us in the power foreordained before the foundations of the world? It is only if we walk through the second veil. If we are going to see our enemies made our footstool, we must commit to a life in the Spirit. In every leadership generation of the twentieth century, God has made provision to take people through this veil. Will He not do the same in the twenty-first century? His first major restoration of the twentieth century came through Azusa Street. God did not quit just because that generation passed the torch of leadership to another. God still made provision in the next generation for those who had yet to walk through the second veil, with an outpouring called the Charismatic Renewal. God began to rain on people that did not really want to get wet, and brought them faithfully through this veil. The third leadership generation of the twentieth century began to emerge in the latter 1980's and once again, the Lord made provision as we saw evangelicals in Europe ablaze with the Holy Spirit. Recent church history (the last hundred years) shows very clearly that God is committed to taking His church through the second veil in their respective generations. Are we willing to march to the tune of our Father's drumbeat?

When the issue of possessing God's mark arises, the process could hardly be seriously initiated without receiving the Holy Spirit. Ephesians 1:13 and 14 says:

> *In Him you also trusted, after you heard the word of truth, the gospel of your salvation; in whom also, having believed, you were sealed with the Holy Spirit of promise, Who is the guarantee of our inheritance until the redemption of the purchased possession, to the praise of His glory.*

The power of the Holy Spirit was obviously intended as a chief mark empowering us to walk out the process. Ephesians 4:30 states: "And do not grieve the Holy Spirit of God, by whom you were sealed for the day of redemption." One might ask, why has God placed such emphasis on the Holy Spirit as the "sealing agent"? Perhaps James 3:8-11 gives the answer:

> *But no man can tame the tongue. It is an unruly evil, full of deadly poison. With it we bless our God and Father, and with it we curse men, who have been made in the similitude of God. Out of the same mouth proceed blessing and cursing. My brethren, these things ought not to be so. Does a spring send forth fresh water and bitter from the same opening?*

Our sealing must begin by first yielding our hearts in salvation in which the Holy Spirit acts as the Agent of conviction, but we must continue to yield the most unruly member, which is our tongue, through a baptism. A multitude of theological excuses are espoused for why one can have the Holy Spirit and not speak in tongues. Every excuse is just a cover for not yielding the tongue. Obey God, not man—the fruit is eternal!

May our hearts

Be fully open,

To the work

You have at hand.

Pliable...contrite

And broken,

Divinely marked

With Holy brand.

The Third and Final Veil

The third and final veil is in Hebrews 10:19-22:

Therefore, brethren, having boldness to enter the Holiest by the blood of Jesus, by a new and living way which He consecrated for us, through the veil, that is, His flesh, and having a High Priest over the house of God, let us draw near with a true heart in full assurance of faith, having our hearts sprinkled from an evil conscience and our bodies washed with pure water.

The Greek word for veil here is **kat-ap-et-as-mah**. It is a compound word. Kata means "to move down or lower one's self" while **pet-om-ahee** is "to spread thoroughly as in preparation to fly." So to be veiled is to have a blanket that comes down over you as you enter a flattened prostrate position.

If Jesus is the pattern, then the pathway through the final veil has a definite Gethsemane flavor, where our flesh yields to the Spirit's leadership. Jesus' body was broken so we could live in the holy of holies. The power of the flesh to dictate must be broken. Jesus lived this pattern for us. The whole issue of brokenness in the New Testament is the process of destroying the power of one's flesh so we are free to move with the Spirit. It is hard to find a group more consumed by flesh in the New Testament than the church at Corinth, yet they were the church that had all the gifts. Through the church in Corinth we see the war between flesh and spirit. 2 Corinthians 6:11

and 7:1 identify the magnitude of warfare we have to face as Paul addressed it at Corinth.

> *Corinthians! We have spoken openly to you, our heart is wide open. You are not restricted by us, but you are restricted by your own affections. Now in return for the same (I speak as to children), you also be open. Do not be unequally yoked together with unbelievers. For what fellowship has righteousness with lawlessness? And what communion has light with darkness? And what accord has Christ with Belial? Or what part has a believer with an unbeliever? And what agreement has the temple of God with idols? For you are the temple of the living God. As God has said: "I will dwell in them And walk among them. I will be their God, And they shall be My people." Therefore "Come out from among them And be separate," says the Lord, "Do not touch what is unclean, And I will receive you. I will be a Father to you, And you shall be My sons and daughters, Says the Lord Almighty." Therefore, having these promises, beloved, let us cleanse ourselves from all filthiness of the flesh and spirit, perfecting holiness in the fear of God.*

Many have perverted this passage in centuries gone by. God's intent was never to "hide away" in a monastery far away from the world. His intent for us was to get free from the dictates of the flesh so we could present Jesus to the world. The third veil is when God comes to us and says, "I am going to give you victory over the dictates of your own flesh, and I am going to lead you into holiness and the fear of the Lord." This is the pathway to realize what Paul prayed in Ephesians 3:14-22:

> *For this reason I bow my knees to the Father of our Lord Jesus Christ, from whom the whole family in heaven and earth is named, that He would grant you, according to the riches of His glory, to be strengthened with might through His Spirit in the inner man, that Christ may dwell in your hearts through faith; that you, being rooted and grounded in love, may be able to comprehend with all the saints what is the width and length and depth and height — to know the*

love of Christ which passes knowledge; that you may be filled with all the fullness of God. Now to Him who is able to do exceedingly abundantly above all that we ask or think, according to the power that works in us, to Him be glory in the church by Christ Jesus throughout all ages, world without end. Amen.

If this is available, why do we not have it? The answer to why we do not have **fullness** may be in Philippians 2:19-21:

*But I trust in the Lord Jesus to send Timothy to you shortly, that I also may be encouraged when I know your state. For I have no one like-minded, who will sincerely care for your state. **For all seek their own, not the things which are of Christ Jesus** (see Purifying the Altar).*

The book of Philippians is one of the last books Paul wrote. He had established many churches during three major missionary journeys. How is it he only has one person he can send? The war with the flesh has many causalities. Only the extremely determined pass through. The veil is the flesh and we should marvel at its strength. The fact Paul only has one he can send, after years of ministry and establishing many churches, speaks volumes about the power of this veil and the warfare necessary to get through it. With Corinth as the example, 1 Corinthians 11 states in verses 23-26:

For I received from the Lord that which I also delivered to you: that the Lord Jesus on the same night in which He was betrayed took bread; and when He had given thanks, He broke it and said, "Take, eat; this is My body which is broken for you; do this in remembrance of Me." In the same manner He also took the cup after supper, saying, "This cup is the new covenant in My blood. This do, as often as you drink it, in remembrance of Me." For as often as you eat this bread and drink this cup, you proclaim the Lord's death till He comes.

One of the mysteries of verse 26 in this passage is, historically, the early church preached resurrection not death. Resurrection was their primary message, and yet Paul says in verse 26:

> *For as often as you eat this bread and drink this cup, you*
> *proclaim the Lord's **death** till He comes.*

Are we to be led through a death?

The progression here is pattern, principle and pathway. Jesus demonstrated all three by walking through that third veil. Verses 27-29 tell us:

> *Therefore whoever eats this bread or drinks this cup of the*
> *Lord in an unworthy manner will be guilty of the body and*
> *blood of the Lord. But let a man examine himself, and so let*
> *him eat of that bread and drink of that cup. For he who eats*
> *and drinks in an unworthy manner eats and drinks*
> *judgment to himself, not discerning the Lord's body.*

When we do not discern the Lord's body, we eat and drink judgment to ourselves. The judgment is obvious. The judgment is verse 30, "For this reason many are weak and sick among you, and many sleep." The judgment was clear: **weak, sick, dead**. Twenty-five years ago, I was taught that judgment in this passage came because we did not discern what was available in the covenant and therefore it was an issue of being destroyed for lack of knowledge. The problem with that interpretation is it does not fit the context of the passage. A primary principle of exegesis asserts, context determines meaning. Verses 31 and 32 make it clear the judgment comes from God. If we judge ourselves, the Lord will not have to judge us, but because we do not judge ourselves over the chief issues outlined, we are judged or chastened by the Lord. And the judgment is: weak, sick, or dead. What principle is so crucial as to require such severe judgment? What is the problem here? Verse 33 states, "Therefore, my brethren, when you come together to eat, wait for one another." That takes us back to verses 20-21:

> *Therefore when you come together in one place, is it not to*
> *eat the Lord's Supper. For in eating, **each one takes his***
> ***own ahead of others....**"*

The veil that is on the flesh in this passage is the issue of selfishness, the absolute antonym for servanthood. They were taking the Lord's Supper, proclaiming the Lord's death, the ultimate message of servanthood and sacrifice for one another, while selfishly and grubbily grabbing the best for themselves. The chief issue, which brought judgment, was **"each one takes—his own...ahead of others."** The problem at Corinth was they had never walked through the third veil. Have we walked through this veil? Do we go to church to serve one another or do we go to church with the same attitude we read that was prevalent at Corinth?

The pathway through the veil is once again mentioned in Philippians 3:14-21. It is revealing to note Paul says in Philippians they were not the enemies of Christ, but "...enemies of the **cross** of Christ." The price tag for going through the veil is the application of the cross. It happens when we encounter a crucifying circumstance or situation. It is at the point of application where we usually fail to discern the purposes of God and often fully resist attempts of the Spirit to complete the cleansing or unveiling. We have whole denominations today demonstrating the thickness of the veil. Many who have been divorced, through no fault of their own, can never stand in the pulpit to preach denominationally. The irony of it is many who pastor those same denominational churches have been blessed at some point by God's outpouring through a divorced minister. God raised up a very fruitful denomination through the apostolic ministry of Aimee McPhearson. That had to be a double hit for pharisaism—she was a divorced woman.

Who but the greatest of the Pharisees can deny multitudes received renewal and a touch of the Holy Spirit at Toronto. Sometimes God judges pharisaism by His choice of leaders. The issue has never been divorce, murder or anything else. The issue has always been: Are we willing to let the tragedy, adversity and pain of personal failure take us through the veil—which is our flesh? A good failure can exceed the value of seminary in ministry. I have seen it prove true many times. That which the Pharisees would say disqualifies for ministry, if it produces brokenness and becomes the catalyst for taking us through the veil, can actually produce our chief qualification for ministry. How can we allow religious spirits to make us so critical? How can we judge as disqualifying factors the very events that in God's eyes qualify based not on the act, but the resultant condition and response of the heart? Pharisaism and law often seem to dominate. Where is grace, mercy and discerning of spirits? (See *The Sure Mercies of David*.)

In 2 Corinthians 4:1-12, Paul outlines the cost of letting the Lord take us through the veil:

> *Therefore, since we have this ministry, as we have received mercy, we do not lose heart. But we have renounced the hidden things of shame, not walking in craftiness nor handling the word of God deceitfully, but by manifestation of the truth commending ourselves to every man's conscience in the sight of God. But even if our gospel is veiled, it is veiled to those who are perishing, whose minds the god of this age has blinded, who do not believe, lest the light of the gospel of the glory of Christ, who is the image of God, should shine on them. For we do not preach ourselves, but Christ Jesus the Lord, and ourselves your servants for Jesus' sake. For it is the God who commanded light to shine out of darkness who has shone in our hearts to give the light of the knowledge of the glory of God in the face of Jesus Christ. But we have this treasure in earthen vessels, that the excellence of the power may be of God and not of us. We are hard pressed on every side, yet not crushed; we are perplexed, but not in despair; persecuted, but not forsaken; struck down, but not destroyed— always carrying about in the body the dying of the Lord Jesus, that the life of Jesus also may be manifested in our body. For we who live are always delivered to death for Jesus' sake, that the life of Jesus also may be manifested in our mortal flesh. So then death is working in us, but life in you.*

We might be tempted to say, "Well, this was just the apostle Paul and it was the pathway God led him through." Unfortunately for us, this is the pathway God led the early church through. That is very clear because Peter speaks of the same thing in 1 Peter 4:1-5. He makes it clear that the third and final veil, the flesh, has to be crucified; and we walk through the crucifixion for one reason, that we "...no longer should live the rest of our time in the flesh for the lusts of men, but for the will of God." That is the purpose for which God takes us through the veil. There is no shortcut. There is no other way. If we are going to receive the **fullness** of God, we have to obtain it on His terms—not our own. The fruit of walking through the third veil is Hebrews 4:8-10:

> *For if Joshua had given them rest, then He would not afterward have spoken of another day. There remains therefore a rest for the people of God. For he who has entered His rest has himself also ceased from his works as God did from His.*

Some equate "entering God's rest" with retirement and Country Club Christianity, but in God there is no retirement. When self-promotion is crucified, rest becomes accessible. We cease from our works only when there is no more self-seeking. And because there is no more seeking our own, we see the fulfillment of the promised rest.

> *Let us therefore be diligent to enter that rest, lest anyone fall after the same example of disobedience. For the word of God is living and powerful, and sharper than any two-edged sword, piercing even to the division of soul and spirit, and of joints and marrow, and is a discerner of the thoughts and intents of the heart. And there is no creature hidden from His sight, but all things are naked and open to the eyes of Him to whom we must give account. Seeing then that we have a great High Priest who has passed through the heavens, Jesus the Son of God, let us hold fast our confession. For we do not have a High Priest who cannot sympathize with our weaknesses, but was in all points tempted as we are, yet without sin. Let us therefore come boldly to the throne of grace, that we may obtain mercy and find grace to help in time of need.*

> *For every high priest taken from among men is appointed for men in things pertaining to God, that he may offer both gifts and sacrifices for sins. He can have compassion on those who are ignorant and going astray, since he himself is also beset by weakness. Because of this he is required as for the people, so also for himself, to offer for sins. And no man takes this honor to himself, but he who is called by God, just as Aaron was. So also Christ did not glorify Himself to*

become High Priest, but it was He who said to Him: "You are My Son, Today I have begotten You." As He also says in another place, "You are a priest forever according to the order of Melchizedek"; who, in the days of His flesh, when He had offered up prayers and supplications, with vehement cries and tears to Him who was able to save Him from death, and was heard because of His godly fear, though He was a Son, yet He learned obedience by the things which He suffered. And having been perfected, He became the author of eternal salvation to all who obey Him, called by God as High Priest "according to the order of Melchizedek...."

Hebrews 4:11-5:10

Rest comes to us because of being wholly given over to God and His purpose. There is no other way to get rest. We have to walk it out on God's chosen path, and the price tag is walking through three veils, obtaining each element of the final marks fully qualifying us to wear God's name on our forehead.

I often say...
that my heart's cry,
is that Christ live
and self may die.

Yet in my
immaturity,
there's much ahead
that I don't see.

And when I truly
face the cross,
I'm unprepared
for this much loss.

There's agony
to fully die,
with groans beyond
the deepest sigh.

Yet Christ —Who's
all the world to me,
beat death's
impossibility.

My hand in His —
my cross I face,
through "death" now to
a better place.

Epilogue

Prayer of Consecration and Commitment

*Father, I come to You
yielding all I have and am —
all future and present assets,
all talents hidden and developed,
all dreams, hopes, desires and visions —
asking that You spend the volume
which comprises my life
in accomplishing Your eternal purposes and plans.*

*I give You the right
to make my life count
for fulfilling Your desires
by spending me in any way You deem necessary
for the eternal good of my family,
community and nation.*

*Let me be one whose life makes an impact
on eternity because
of what You ordained me to do on earth.
I choose to sow future days, months and years
into purchasing Your purposes and plans
including filling the cup, in order to
birth a new "heavens and earth."
Let my life praise Your Name!*

Footnotes

1 Richard Frances Weymouth, *The New Testament in Modern Speech*, (London. James Clarke and Co., 3rd edition 1911), p. 733.

2 Ibid., p. 344.

3 Spiros Zodiates Th.D., *The Complete Word Study Dictionary: New Testament* (Copyright 1992 by AMG International, Inc. revised edition, copyright 1993) pp. 577, 1199, 1200.

4 The Discipleship Movement had a noble goal but quickly deteriorated when mammon entered through tithing upstream. This opened the door to abuse and ever-increasing control.

5 Al Houghton, *Purifying the Altar*, Word at Work Ministries, Inc., 2007. Available on request. WAW Inc., P.O. Box 366, Placentia, CA 92871 or by phone (714) 693-3033 or wordatwork.org.

6 "Anointing to Spoil" series, Word At Work Ministries, Inc., copyright 1988, 1989, 1994. Series outlining God's prophetic plan for businesses used to finance end-time harvest. Available on request.

7 *Gesenius' Hebrew-Chaldee Lexicon to the Old Testament*, (Baker Book House, Grand Rapids, MI, Translated by Samuel Prideaux Tregelles, LL.D. Copyright 1979, 1st printed 1857 Samuel Bagster and Sons, p. 857.

8 *Theological Dictionary of the New Testament* Vol. VI, pp. 283-304, edited by Gerhard Kittel, Translator and Editor Geoffrey Bromiley, D.LITT., D.D. (Copyright 1968 by Wm. B. Eerdmans Publishing Co. Reprinted Nov. 1983), pp. 283-304.

9 Spiros Zodhiates, Th.D., *The Complete Word Study New Testament*, (copyright 1991 by AMG International, Inc., 2nd edition 1992, AMG Publishers, Chattanooga, TN 37422), "Lexical Aids to the New Testament," pp. 892, 893.

10 Alexander Balmain Bruce, D.D., *The Expositor's Greek Testament*, edited by W. Robertson Nicoll, M.A., LL.D. Vol. I, (Wm. B. Eerdmans Publishing Co., Grand Rapids, MI, Aug. 1983), p. 188.

11 *American Dictionary of the English Language*, Noah Webster 1828. Noah Webster's First Edition of an American Dictionary of the English Language. Published by the Foundation for American Christian Education. Copyright 1967.

12 *Theological Wordbook of the Old Testament*, Harris, Archer and Waltke, Vol. 1, copyright 1980, Moody Press, Chicago, IL. p. 57.

13 *Gesenius' Hebrew-Chaldee Lexicon To The Old Testament* (Baker Book House, Grand Rapids, MI, Translated by Samuel Prideaux Tregelles, LL.D. (1979), 1st printed 1857 Samuel Bagster and Sons.

14 *Logos Bible Software X*, Enhanced Strong's Lexicon, Scholar's Library Gold, Logos Bible Software, 1313 Commercial Street, Bellingham, WA 98225-4307.

15 *The Ante-Nicene Fathers*, American Reprint of The Edinburgh Edition, Vol. III, Introduction, (Wm. B. Eerdmans Publishing, Grand Rapids, MI. Reprinted Dec. 1986) p. 3.

16 Ibid, Vol. III, p. 638.

17 Ibid, Vol. IV, p. 196.

18 Ibid, Vol. V, pp. 303, 304.

Bibliography

A Linguistic Key to the Greek New Testament by Fritz Rienecker and Cleon Rogers. Copyright 1976, 1980 by The Zondervan Corporation, Grand Rapids, MI 49530. Used by permission of Zondervan Publishing House.

Biblical definitions from Alexander Balmain Bruce, D.D., *The Expositor's Greek Testament,* edited by W. Robertson Nicoll, M.A., LL.D. in Vol. I, copyright 1983. Used by permission of Wm. B. Eerdmans Publishing Co., 255 Jefferson Avenue SE, Grand Rapids, MI 49503 USA.

Biblical definitions from *The Theological Dictionary of the New Testament,* Vol. VI, edited by Gerhard Kittel and Gerherd Friedrich, translated by Geoffrey Bromiley as the foundation for definition of Greek words used. Used by permission of Wm. B. Eerdmans Publishing Co., 225 Jefferson Avenue SE, Grand Rapids, MI 49503 USA.

Definition taken from *American Dictionary of the English Language,* Noah Webster 1828. Noah Webster's First Edition of an American Dictionary of the English Language. Published by the Foundation for American Christian Education. Copyright 1967.

Gesenius' Hebrew-Chaldee Lexicon to the Old Testament, (Baker Book House, Grand Rapids, MI, Translated by Samuel Prideaux Tregelles, LL.D. (Copyright 1979, 1st printing 1857 Samuel Bagster and Sons).

Greek Text used: 21st edition of *Eberhard Nestle's Novum Testamentum Graece.*

Richard Frances Weymouth, *The New Testament in Modem Speech,* London. (James Clarke and Co., 3rd edition, copyright 1911).

Spiros Zodhiates, Th.D, *The Complete Word Study Dictionary.* New Testament (copyright 1992 by AMG International, Inc., Revised edition, 1993, Chattanooga, TN 37422).

Spiros Zodhiates, Th.D., *The Complete Word Study New Testament,* (copyright 1991 by AMG International, Inc., 2nd Edition 1992, AMG Publishers, Chattanooga, TN 37422) "Lexical Aids to the New Testament."

The Ante-Nicene Fathers, American Reprint of the Edinburgh Edition, in the Introduction of Vol. III, p. 638, Vol. IV, p. 196 and Vol. V, pp. 303, 304. Used by permission of Wm. B. Eerdmans Publishing Co., 255 Jefferson Avenue SE, Grand Rapids, MI 49503 USA.

About the Author

Al Houghton grew up in a small town in Missouri. He graduated from the University of Missouri at Columbia with a Bachelor of Science degree in Marketing. After graduation, he joined the Navy to become a pilot, flying 161 combat reconnaissance missions during the Vietnam War. He left the military to fly commercially, but God dramatically intervened, calling him into ministry.

In 1975, he moved to Southern California to attend seminary and earned a Master of Divinity degree in theology. Immediately upon graduation, the Lord instructed him to start a teaching ministry and live by faith.

The teaching ministry began in home Bible studies, but grew to occupy other facilities like Mott Auditorium on the campus of the U.S. Center for World Missions in Pasadena, where Al taught for ten years.

Doors opened in other nations and Al began to minister at International Leadership Conferences from 1984 through 1987 which marked a transition as God added a prophetic touch to his teaching ministry.

A daily Bible study, entitled the "Word at Work," was begun in 1981 and over two decades of daily Bible studies can be downloaded at wordatwork.org.

Al's current assignment is elevating the Church into their kingly priesthood as "agents of justice." Many free nations stand at the crossroads of judgment or salvation based on choices made. By invoking the covenant of "Sure Mercies," the Church can impact those choices. Only a vibrant church who knows their covenant can confront political leaders in the power of the Spirit. Saving the nation means awakening the Church to the power of their covenantal roots!

To place an order, log onto:
wordatwork.org

Or you can write to us at:
P. O. Box 366, Placentia, CA 92871

THE SURE MERCIES OF DAVID

How should believers respond to the avalanche of evil assaulting our nation, cursing our biblical culture and outlawing the voices of virtue?

God covenanted with David to redeem his failure and cut off his enemies. David knew what to ask for to save his land, based on this covenant. Jesus guaranteed the covenant of "Sure Mercy" and Paul preached it in Acts 13 with a warning that failure to use it could cost the loss of cities, and even the nation.

"Sure Mercy" empowers the church by putting a two-edged sword in the hand of every believer. The first edge cuts away the guilt, shame and insecurity of personal failure allowing God to transform the failure into a foundation for future prophetic fulfillment. The second edge moves God's hand to execute biblical justice saving the nation from all those intent on perverting and destroying the land by filling it with iniquity!

Learning the difference between "Sure Mercy" for an individual and "Sure Mercy" for a nation empowers us to pray an entirely different way. David expressed in the Psalms God's heart for victory and His willingness to war in our behalf. This book helps the church war spiritually as David did physically!

Purifying the Altar

S ome of the most amazing covenantal promises in Scripture concern money and how we handle it. If we pass the mammon test, we can participate in spiritual government. Without cleansing the temple, the authority for spiritual government is lost.

The only place in Scripture where God invites us to **put Him to the test** is in the context of our choices with money. Malachi 3:10 states,

"Bring all the tithes into the storehouse...."

By emphasizing the personal choice of giving as the determinant covenant factor, we have missed half of what the Bible teaches on this subject, and consequently closed the windows of heaven. *Purifying the Altar* offers a path parting the waters of tradition and pursuing an open heaven.

Jesus stated in Matthew 23, *"Fools and blind! For which is greater, the gift or the altar that sanctifies the gift?"* Jesus made the condition of the altar the determinant covenant factor. When an altar is cleansed so that it "sanctifies" what is given, the windows of heaven open because the covenant is actually consummated.

Purifying the Altar is a study of the biblical principles which contribute to closing or opening the windows of heaven through purifying both the personal and corporate altars!

The following questions are answered:

1 What transpires in the realm of the spirit when we do business with God at an impure altar?

2 In every Bible-believing congregation the majority of people agree, "We tithe and are doing the best we know to do, but we do not see the windows of heaven opened to the full extent God promised." Why?

3 The spiritual law of the altar states, the condition of the altar where we attend, participate and put our money, is reproduced in our lives whether we are aware of it or not.

CONVERTS
or DISCIPLES?

Converts or Disciples? is a prophetic word to the church, hopefully causing a reassessment of our ultimate purpose. If our number one goal is making disciples, then every believer we impact should be empowered to pass the 12-fold test of discipleship reflecting the commitment of the early church as they cultivated an apostolic culture!

A Prophetic Word to the American Church

CONVERTS *or* DISCIPLES?

The 12-fold Test of Discipleship

1. True discipleship begins when we choose to embrace _____.
2. Converts walk where _____ _____, while disciples walk where ____ .
3. A convert sets his own _____, while a disciple embraces God's _____.
4. Converts often reject a _____ _____, while disciples accept it.
5. Converts use faith to _____ _____, while disciples use it to _____ _____.
6. Converts are oblivious to _____, while disciples discern it.
7. Disciples volunteer for _____, while converts hesitate.
8. Disciples dare not covenant with _____, but converts do it repeatedly.
9. Disciples are vigilant about who their actions _____, but converts are not.
10. Disciples escape financial manipulation because they give only by _____ need, while converts usually respond to _____ need.
11. Disciples display the _____ _____ _____ _____, while converts do not.
12. Disciples have to extend _____, while converts think it is optional.